Anxiety Disorders

THE STATE OF
MENTAL ILLNESS
AND ITS THERAPY

THE STATE OF
MENTAL ILLNESS
AND ITS THERAPY

Anxiety Disorders

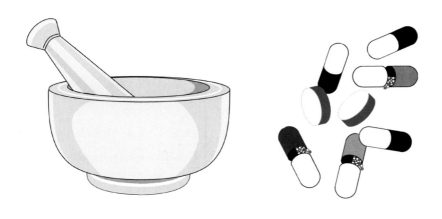

Shirley Brinkerhoff

Mason Crest

Mason Crest
450 Parkway Drive, Suite D
Broomall, PA 19008
www.masoncrest.com

Printed in the Hashemite Kingdom of Jordan.

First printing
9 8 7 6 5 4 3 2 1

Series ISBN: 978-1-4222-2819-7
ISBN: 978-1-4222-2821-0
ebook ISBN: 978-1-4222-8982-2

The Library of Congress has cataloged the
        hardcopy format(s) as follows:

        Library of Congress Cataloging-in-Publication Data

Brinkerhoff, Shirley.
  [Drug therapy and anxiety disorders]
  Anxiety disorders / Shirley Brinkerhoff.
      pages cm. – (The state of mental illness and its therapy)
  Audience: Age 12.
  Audience: Grade 7 to 8.
  Revision of: Drug therapy and anxiety disorders. 2004.
  Includes bibliographical references and index.
  ISBN 978-1-4222-2821-0 (hardcover) – ISBN 978-1-4222-2819-7 (series) – ISBN 978-1-4222-8982-2
(ebook)
  1. Anxiety disorders–Juvenile literature. 2. Anxiety disorders–Treatment–Juvenile literature. 3.
Psychotropic drugs–Side effects–Juvenile literature. I. Title.
  RC531.B758 2014
  616.85'220651–dc23
                        2013007678

Produced by Vestal Creative Services.

www.vestalcreative.com

Picture Credits:
Artville: pp. 17, 18, 20, 39, 44, 46, 52, 67, 72, 77, 88, 91, 112. Benjamin Stewart: pp. 13, 33, 56, 85. Corbis: pp. 108, 115, 123. Filmfoto | Dreamstime.com: p. 121 Image Source: pp. 54, 58. Jovani Carlo Gorospe | Dreamstime.com: p. 41. PhotoDisc: pp. 30, 48, 49, 60, 63, 71, 73, 75, 78, 90, 94, 96, 101, 103, 104, 106, 117, 119. Ponsulak | Dreamstime.com: p. 51. Robert Hambley | Dreamstime.com: p. 26. Rubberball: pp. 10, 23, 26. Sebastian Czapnik | Dreamstime.com: p. 21. Showface | Dreamstime.com: p. 46. Sijohnsen | Dreamstime.com: p. 110. Skypixel | Dreamstime.com: p. 80. Stephanie Swartz | Dreamstime.com: p. 43. Stockbyte: pp. 15, 24, 38, 89. Stratum | Dreamstime.com: p. 105. Trottola | Dreamstime.com: p. 116 Ultrapop | Dreamstime.com: p. 98. The individuals in these images are models, and the images are for illustrative purposes only. The individuals in these images are models, and the images are for illustrative purposes only. To the best knowledge of the publisher, all other images are in the public domain. If any image has been inadvertently uncredited or miscredited, please notify Vestal Creative Services, Vestal, New York 13850, so that rectification can be made for future printings.

CONTENTS

Introduction
by Mary Ann McDonnell

Teenagers have reason to be interested in psychiatric disorders and their treatment. Friends, family members, and even teens themselves may experience one of these disorders. Using scenarios adolescents will understand, this series explains various psychiatric disorders and the drugs that treat them.

Diagnosis and treatment of psychiatric disorders in children between six and eighteen years old are well studied and documented in the scientific journals. A paper appearing in the *Journal of the American Academy of Child and Adolescent Psychiatry* in 2010 estimated that 49.5 percent of all adolescents aged 13 to 18 were affected by at least one psychiatric disorder. Various other studies have reported similar findings. Needless to say, many children and adolescents are suffering from psychiatric disorders and are in need of treatment.

Many children have more than one psychiatric disorder, which complicates their diagnoses and treatment plans. Psychiatric disorders often occur together. For instance, a person with a sleep disorder may also be depressed; a teenager with attention-deficit/hyperactivity disorder (ADHD) may also have a substance-use disorder. In psychiatry, we call this comorbidity. Much research addressing this issue has led to improved diagnosis and treatment.

The most common child and adolescent psychiatric disorders are anxiety disorders, depressive disorders, and ADHD. Sleep disorders, sexual disorders, eating disorders, substance-abuse disorders, and psychotic disorders are also quite common. This series has volumes that address each of these disorders.

Major depressive disorders have been the most commonly diagnosed mood disorders for children and adolescents. Researchers don't agree as to how common mania and bipolar disorder are in children. Some experts believe that manic episodes in children and adolescents are underdiagnosed. Many times, a mood disturbance may occur with another psychiatric disorder. For instance, children with ADHD may also be depressed. ADHD is just one psychiatric disorder that is a major health concern for children, adolescents, and adults. Studies of ADHD have reported prevalence rates among children that range from two to 12 percent.

Failure to understand or seek treatment for psychiatric disorders puts children and young adults at risk of developing substance-use disorders. For example, recent research indicates that those with ADHD who were treated with medication were 85 percent less likely to develop a substance-use disorder. Results like these emphasize the importance of timely diagnosis and treatment.

Early diagnosis and treatment may prevent these children from developing further psychological problems. Books like those in this series provide important information, a vital first step toward increased awareness of psychological disorders; knowledge and understanding can shed light on even the most difficult subject. These books should never, however, be viewed as a substitute for professional consultation. Psychiatric testing and an evaluation by a licensed professional is recommended to determine the needs of the child or adolescent and to establish an appropriate treatment plan.

Foreword
by Donald Esherick

We live in a society filled with technology—from computers surfing the Internet to automobiles operating on gas and batteries. In the midst of this advanced society, diseases, illnesses, and medical conditions are treated and often cured with the administration of drugs, many of which were unknown thirty years ago. In the United States, we are fortunate to have an agency, the Food and Drug Administration (FDA), which monitors the development of new drugs and then determines whether the new drugs are safe and effective for use in human beings.

When a new drug is developed, a pharmaceutical company usually intends that drug to treat a single disease or family of diseases. The FDA reviews the company's research to determine if the drug is safe for use in the population at large and if it effectively treats the targeted illnesses. When the FDA finds that the drug is safe and effective, it approves the drug for treating that specific disease or condition. This is called the labeled indication.

During the routine use of the drug, the pharmaceutical company and physicians often observe that a drug treats other medical conditions besides what is indicated in the labeling. While the labeling will not include the treatment of the particular condition, a physician can still prescribe the drug to a patient with this disease. This is known as an unlabeled or off-label indication. This series contains information about both the labeled and off-label indications of psychiatric drugs.

I have reviewed the books in this series from the perspective of the pharmaceutical industry and the FDA, specifically focusing on the labeled indications, uses, and known side effects of these drugs. Further information can be found on the FDA's website (www.FDA. gov).

Anxious feelings can make us feel restless, nervous, and worried. They can be caused by many factors: life circumstances, diet, and physical condition. Everyone feels anxious sometimes, but anxiety disorders are far more extreme, involving anxious feelings for which there is no apparent reason.

Chapter One

Those Who Suffer from Anxiety Disorders

Anxiety disorders are the single most common psychiatric illnesses in North America. Estimates are that up to 15 percent of Americans will suffer from an anxiety disorder at some time. Since almost everyone feels anxious now and then, it's important to distinguish between anxiety disorders and normal anxiety. In her book *Mental Health Concepts and Techniques*, Mary Beth Early defines anxiety as a state of tension and uneasiness. Anxious feelings from time to time are normal, even useful, parts of daily life. We say we have the "jitters," or the "willies," or that another person is nervous.

Sometimes anxious feelings can result from simple physical causes, such as eating and drinking things that contain caffeine or large quantities of sugar. Tobacco and alcohol can also cause changes in anxiety levels. (For more information on the relationship of caffeine, sugar, tobacco, and alcohol to anxiety, see chapter seven, "Alternative and Supplementary Treatments.")

Anxiety can be a positive thing that helps us to avoid harm. Jack M. Gorman comments in *The New Psychiatry* that anxiety makes us fear the consequences of not checking the kitchen when we smell smoke, of not studying for an exam, or of not paying our taxes to the IRS. Anxious feelings can help get us ready to face difficulties or challenges, and sometimes even emergencies. Walter B. Cannon, an American physiologist, was the first to identify what he called the "fight-or-flight" reaction, our body's response to emergency situations. This response includes a sudden increase in heart rate, breathing rate, and blood pressure, and also an increase in blood flow to muscles. These physical changes are all meant to allow a person to either flee or fight in the face of danger.

It has long been recognized among performing artists that a little anxiety helps put an "edge" on a performance, driving the artist to do a bit better than would be possible without it. Now, scientific measurements of blood flow in the brain using modern brain-imaging techniques show that low levels of anxiety cause an increase in brain activity. Students who are a little worried about an upcoming test actually have a better ability to concentrate and retain information. Large amounts of anxiety have just the opposite effect on the brain, however. Some people talk about "freezing up" when they take a test or give a speech, and that may be an apt expression, since brain activity seems to decrease in the presence of excessive anxiety.

Unlike these reasonable kinds of worry, which are linked to specific situations such as performance or possible danger, anxiety disorders involve anxious feelings for which there is apparently no reason at all. In psychiatric terms, this abnormal state of anxiety is characterized by the feeling of powerlessness and the inability to cope with threatening events, typically imaginary, and by physical tension evidenced by sweating, trembling, and other **physiological** reactions.

When anxious feelings grow so strong that they interfere with normal functioning, they need to be checked out by medical professionals who can diagnose and treat anxiety disorders. The stories that follow can help you understand what true anxiety disorders are.

Cassie McCauley

When terrorists attacked the World Trade Center on September 11, 2001, Cassie McCauley watched in horror from her classroom on the New Jersey side of the Hudson River. Her heart pounded faster and faster as she saw billowing clouds of dark gray smoke pour from the landmark buildings, and when the first tower collapsed, she began feeling light-headed. By the time the second tower fell in on itself, Cassie was so nauseated and dizzy she had to sit down until the feeling passed. Along with millions across North America and around the world, Cassie grieved for the families who lost relatives and friends. But she never anticipated how much trouble September 11th would cause in her own life.

Cassie's school closed down for the remainder of that week, then reopened the Monday after the attack. It was on that Monday that Cassie first noticed the strange feelings. As she walked up the concrete steps to the double doors of the school, a feeling of **foreboding** swept over her, as though something terrible was about to happen. The feeling was so strong that she turned on the top step and nervously scanned the sky over the

physiological: Pertaining to the body's functioning.

foreboding: An omen or feeling that something is going to happen, often something bad or evil.

Hudson River. She saw nothing unusual. Yet her feet refused to move when she tried to enter the school building, and the nausea and dizziness she'd felt while watching the attack returned.

Through sheer willpower, Cassie finally forced herself to enter the school, but her heart was pounding so hard she had to sit down the minute she arrived at her first class. Fortunately, she was early and few of her friends had arrived yet. She put her head down on her desk and took slow, deep breaths until her heart rate slowed down and the nausea passed.

For the next week, Cassie worried that the panicky feelings might return, scared that she might lose control around her friends. But by the time the weekend came around, Cassie was laughing at herself. A lot of worrying over nothing, that's what she'd been doing. Whatever had happened on the school steps on Monday morning, it was gone now, probably just some kind of delayed reaction to the terrorist attack.

Then Cassie and her boyfriend Brian got into an argument while eating at a local fast-food restaurant. Brian suggested they postpone other plans to see a new movie together on Saturday night. Cassie objected, and before she quite realized what was happening, they were shouting angry words at each other in the car on the way home. Almost immediately, the feeling of danger returned. Cassie's heart began racing—she could feel it pounding inside her chest—and waves of nausea and dizziness came over her again.

After that, Cassie never knew when another attack would happen. She experienced the same symptoms a week later when a teacher criticized an assignment she'd handed in. It happened again when she went with her mother to shop at a busy department store one Saturday and then on a Sunday afternoon when she and Brian tried to exit a college stadium after a crowded football game.

Within a few weeks, the attacks were coming more and more often, and Cassie began feeling like a prisoner of whatever it was that was wrong with her. Too embarrassed to explain her symptoms to her parents or friends, she "created" an imaginary case of intestinal flu and stayed home from school for nearly two weeks, spending

Teenagers often experience anxiety for a variety of reasons. Sometimes their symptoms may be dismissed as typical adolescent behaviors, rather than as signs of a psychiatric disorder.

Interestingly, anxiety is an emotion common not only to people but even to some animals. Anxiety can be found in nearly every category of human psychiatric illness, with social deviancy (also called antisocial personality) being the sole exception—and even some deviant individuals have reported tension and discomfort in knowing they differ from other humans.

most of the time alone in her bedroom. She made excuses to cancel dates with Brian and told her mother she was simply too busy making up schoolwork to go shopping again just now. Even so, the strange sense of foreboding, the racing pulse, and the nausea all began to invade even the safety of her room.

One morning, when Cassie told her father she was still too sick to return to school, he put his foot down. "Cassie, I don't know what's going on with you, but this doesn't make any sense. You're eating fine, the doctor says he can't find anything wrong with you, and I just don't think you really have the flu."

The look of concern on his face made Cassie feel sick with guilt at the way she'd been lying, and the awful sense of foreboding swept over her again. She knew what was coming next.

"I can't talk now," she stammered. "I really can't—please—I'm sorry." She rushed back to her bedroom and dropped to the bed, bent over, head to her knees, to make the room stop spinning.

A half an hour later, the attack had passed, and Cassie was curled up in the corner of the living room couch, tears running down her face. She had no idea what could possibly be wrong with her, but it was ruining her life. She was going to fail all her classes if this kept up, and the very thought terrified her. How would she ever get into college if she couldn't complete this year? How could she ever explain to her parents and to Brian what was happening?

Other questions raced through her mind. Could she be having

a mental breakdown? Even worse, could she have a brain tumor? Maybe that would explain the dizziness. But what about the sense of foreboding? What if that meant she really did have a brain tumor, and her body was trying to signal her that something was terribly wrong?

Cassie's father sat down beside her, his arm around her shoulder. "Cassie," he said, "I don't know what's going on here, but whatever it is, I think it's time to talk it over. Let your mother and me in on what's really going on. Please."

Cassie's parents made an appointment with a psychiatrist for her, and she was glad to have them both along as she went through the examination. Cassie found out that she was experiencing the symptoms of an anxiety disorder known as panic disorder. Panic disorder is one of several different types of anxiety disorders, and although the disorders have similarities, each has individual symptoms and requires different medications and treatments.

Trevor Anhalt

Whereas Cassie's attacks occurred without warning, seemingly unconnected to any specific trigger event, Trevor Anhalt's terror of flying overwhelmed him every time he even thought about getting on an airplane. He'd always been afraid of planes but had managed so far to talk his parents out of any family vacation that involved flying. Then, one day shortly after his sixteenth birthday, Trevor popped the top of his soda can and glanced at the inside of the tab. "Congratulations! You have won a trip for four to Hawaii!" the message proclaimed. He ran through the house, shouting the news to his parents and older sister. Later, however, he read the small print, which said that transportation via United Airlines was included, and he realized he had a problem. Suddenly, Trevor had to face his fear of flying head on.

Trevor's sister had gotten on the phone immediately when she

Most people might feel a little nervous waiting alone on a dark street at night. But for a person whose anxiety disorder centers around fear of the dark or fear of city streets, this experience could be emotionally and even physically overwhelming.

heard the news, telling all her friends about the upcoming trip; soon the news of Trevor's win was all over school. Trevor was the envy of all the other students, who were constantly asking him when he was going to cash in on his prize, but he didn't dare to even think about the trip. The mental picture of himself on an airplane made him light-headed; just the idea made the room seem to spin so violently that he had to hold on to a piece of furniture to stay upright. He struggled against his feelings, telling himself he could conquer this if he simply had more willpower. Eventually, though, even hearing an airplane in the sky overhead could produce the same symptoms.

Trevor's fear of flying was causing plenty of problems in his family. His mother and sister had already begun buying beach clothes and making extravagant plans for their trip to the islands when Trevor finally admitted he couldn't go, and why.

"So call the soda company and tell them that the three of us will go without you!" his sister said.

"I already suggested that to them, actually," Trevor confessed. "But they told me that if the winner doesn't go, the trip is off. It's something about contest regulations." His sister flounced out of the room and slammed the door. She refused to speak to him for the next three weeks.

Things felt strained with his mother and father, too, although they tried to act understanding. "You know," his mother said wistfully, "you'll have to face this fear of flying someday, Trevor. Perhaps now would be as good a time as any . . ."

At last, Trevor couldn't stand the tension at home any longer and went to see his doctor. The doctor listened carefully, then recommended a visit to a therapist, where Trevor was diagnosed as having a specific phobia, situational type, another type of anxiety disorder.

Charlene Williams

Charlene Williams had another kind of problem. Charlene had been outgoing and sociable as a child. Some of her family's favorite sto-

A person with an anxiety disorder may feel as though he is walking a tightrope that may snap at any moment. For him, the world is a dangerous and precarious place.

ries involved tales of Charlene's **gregarious- ness**. As a preschooler, she would charm complete strangers with her bright smile and blond curly hair as she sat in the grocery cart while her mother shopped; often she spontaneously invited these strangers home to dinner, much to her mother's embarrassment.

As Charlene moved into middle school, however, several things happened that made her begin to doubt herself. One of the most popular soccer players on the school team

gregariousness: Liking companionship, being social, outgoing.

Travel is a normal part of many people's business and recreational lives. Someone who has a phobia about flying will find his life restricted by his fears.

liked her for a few weeks, but when they broke up after an argument, hateful graffiti using her name began appearing around school. Charlene was mortified when she saw groups of guys reading the graffiti and laughing. She ran for student council but was defeated soundly. After that, Charlene seemed to lose whatever confidence remained.

Something began changing inside her. Charlene began feeling uneasy in face-to-face social situations at school. She was unable to shake the feeling that other students were sizing her up, and she was sure that their opinion was always negative. She began finding it harder and harder to make eye contact with other students in her class, or with her teachers.

Giving oral reports and presentations had been simple for Charlene before, but now they became a nightmare. The entire time she was speaking, Charlene worried that everyone in the room was judging her appearance, speech, and actions. Her pulse speeded up and she worried that she might pass out.

Then, for the first time in her life, she completely lost her train of thought in the middle of a speech—part of a group presentation that counted as an exam grade for each member of the group. Charlene struggled for several minutes to remember what she was saying and was able to go on only after an embarrassingly long pause, during which other students began fidgeting uneasily in their chairs and clearing their throats. What she said after the pause was disorganized and poorly explained.

"You're just going to have to home school me!" Charlene said to her parents that evening, tears of shame and frustration running down her cheeks. "Everybody in my group is getting a terrible grade, all because of me. I can't even give a simple speech anymore, not to mention just talking to friends. And I don't even understand what's happening to me!"

A person with an anxiety disorder will have physical symptoms as well as emotional; her heart will beat faster, and she may feel faint, sweaty, and nauseated.

Anxiety Disorders

Since anxious feelings are experienced by nearly everyone at one time or another, some people assume that an anxiety disorder is not a serious condition. But if anxious feelings grow so strong that they interfere with daily functioning at work, school, or in relationships, as they did with Cassie McCauley, Trevor Anhalt, or Charlene

A person who has a phobia about social situations may perceive others as unfriendly or even threatening.

Williams, and if this problem lasts for six months or more, it is important to seek professional help. True anxiety disorders can be very serious and, at times, **incapacitating** for many people.

incapacitating: Making it impossible to do something.

A person with generalized anxiety disorder will worry about many things; she may be exhausted and have difficulty sleeping, but often there will be no real cause for her anxiety.

Chapter Two

Defining Anxiety Disorders

When Tara won a promotion to vice president of her company at the age of thirty-seven, her friends and family threw a huge party for her. While everyone else was congratulating her for her achievement, however, Tara was already beginning to feel anxious. What if she couldn't do the job? Maybe the president had chosen her just because she always portrayed herself as confident, but maybe that was a lie. What if her coworkers were angry that she'd been promoted and they hadn't?

Although Tara had graduated third in her senior class and with highest honors in her Master's in Business Administration program, she now began to worry that she would perform so poorly in her new position that she would ultimately be fired. "Then we'd lose the house!" she cried to her husband Barry a few weeks after her promotion. "You know we can't keep this house on just your salary."

Barry was not only embarrassed by her comment, he was also angered by the apparent senselessness of her constant fretting. "Tara, would you just quit, already?" he said. "It's like lately you're on a fishing expedition for compliments all the time. I'll say it one more time, then that's it: You're smart, Tara. You're the best at what you do. In fact, you're so smart and so good, you make more money than me. There! Are you happy now?"

Stunned by Barry's total lack of understanding, Tara grew more upset than ever. She began sleeping in the guest room because Barry complained that she kept him awake all night with her tossing and turning.

I want to sleep as much as you do, Tara thought wearily. But there were meetings to face the next day—meetings she was in charge of now, and she had to spend those quiet hours in bed rehearsing every word, planning every action, over and over. And yet, even that wasn't enough to help her get rid of her constant dread that soon someone would find out she couldn't do this job. And now, added to all that was the dread that Barry would leave her, too. The more she worried about it all, the tenser her muscles grew.

After a few weeks of trying to function with very little sleep, Tara was desperate for rest, but her back and neck were so tense that they ached constantly. Maybe a glass of wine before bed would help. Maybe two would be better.

In the DSM-IV-TR, criteria for ruling out other disorders are also listed. As an example, GAD would not be diagnosed if the patient's worrying was found to be caused by another disorder, such as Social Phobia or Obsessive-Compulsive Disorder. (Although Obsessive-Compulsive Disorder is listed and briefly defined here, it is dealt with at length in another book in the series The State of Mental Illness and Its Therapy.)

Anxiety Disorders

- Generalized anxiety disorder (GAD)
- Posttraumatic stress disorder (PTSD)
- Obsessive-compulsive disorder (OCD)
- Panic disorder (with or without agoraphobia)
- Specific phobia
- Social phobia or social anxiety disorder (SAD)

Unlike the "good" type of anxiety described in chapter 1, anxiety like Tara's only harms the people that suffer from it. When she finally consults a doctor about her problems, it will become evident that Tara has been something of a "worrier" all her life, though her worries seem to have no basis. She was always an excellent student, far above average, and more than competent at her job. Her husband, though irritated by her present behavior and chafing under the embarrassment that she earns more money than he does, has no intention of leaving her. He is, in fact, deeply committed to her and to making their marriage work, and he tells her that frequently. Until Tara's generalized anxiety disorder (GAD) is diagnosed and she gets help in the form of medication or therapy, however, she'll find that she simply cannot stop worrying on her own. GAD often leads to problems with alcohol and depression, as is already beginning to happen in Tara's case, compounding the problem even further.

Tara's GAD is only one of six recognized anxiety disorders, each requiring specific diagnosis and treatment. Following is a brief description of the different anxiety disorders, with a definition and symptoms listed for each adapted from the *Diagnostic and Statistical Manual of Mental Disorders* Text Revision (DSM-IV-TR), the most recent classification of mental disorders by the American Psychiatric Association.

A person with GAD who lives near a nuclear reactor might worry constantly about nuclear accidents or other catastrophes.

Generalized
Anxiety Disorder [GAD]

Generalized anxiety disorder is a type of excessive anxiety that lasts for at least six months, more days than not, with no reasonable cause. It may occur even when the sufferer's life is going very well. GAD may include chronic feelings of restlessness, difficulty concentrating, tiring easily, irritability, muscle tension, and difficulty in sleeping.

Individuals with GAD find it difficult to control their worry, are distressed by their condition, and find the anxiety they feel keeps them from functioning as well as they otherwise could in their work, school, or social situations. The things they worry about are everyday, routine life circumstances, including finances, health (their own or that of family members), misfortune to children, job responsibilities (present or anticipated), household chores, and car repairs. Children who suffer from GAD typically worry about their own ability to perform, particularly in areas such as school or sporting events, and about catastrophic events, including war, terrorist attacks, or earthquakes. During the time an individual has GAD, worry may shift from one concern to another. Women are diagnosed with GAD more often than men.

People with GAD frequently experience aches and pains, such as stomachache, backache, and headache. For females, menstrual cramps are included. Trembling, twitching, and "feeling shaky" are also reported, as well as sweating, nausea, diarrhea, and an exaggerated startle response.

chronic: Lasting a long time or recurring often.

startle response: Response to surprise, fright, alarm.

Often, people with GAD have felt anxious or nervous for their entire lives, but onset of GAD after age twenty is not unusual. People who are generally more anxious than others often come from families where this trait is prevalent.

PANIC DISORDER

Panic disorder is an anxiety disorder distinguished by recurrent, unexpected panic attacks, such as Cassie McCauley had, followed by a persistent concern (which lasts for a minimum of one month) about having another panic attack. A panic attack is defined as a period of intense fear or discomfort where specific symptoms, which develop suddenly and reach a peak within ten minutes, are present. These symptoms include the following:

- palpitations (rapid beating or fluttering of the heart), pounding heart
- accelerated heart rate
- sweating
- trembling or shaking
- sensations of shortness of breath/smothering
- feeling of choking
- chest pain or discomfort
- nausea/abdominal distress
- feeling dizzy, unsteady, light-headed, or faint
- derealization (feelings of unreality) or depersonalization (detachment from self)
- fear of losing control or going crazy
- fear of dying
- parasthesias (numbness or tingling sensations)
- chills or hot flashes

A minimum of four of these symptoms must be present to qualify an episode as a panic attack.

People with panic disorder often fear that their attacks indicate they have some undiagnosed, life-threatening disease, and they may be unconvinced by medical tests that show this is not the case.

Panic Disorder with Agoraphobia

Panic Disorder without Agoraphobia

Panic disorders are more common in women than in men. Three times as many women as men have panic disorder with agoraphobia; two times as many women as men have panic disorder without agoraphobia.

Such fears may lead the individual to make repeated visits to doctors and emergency rooms—even to the extent of missing so much work that their jobs are endangered. Individuals with this disorder may also be far less tolerant of medication side effects; they may require repeated reassurances in order to continue taking their medication. Other people fear their panic attacks show they are losing their minds or are emotionally weak.

Disruptions in interpersonal relationships, such as leaving home to live independently or getting a divorce, may bring on (or significantly worsen) panic disorder. When this happens, many individuals become discouraged or unhappy about carrying on with their normal routines; they may consider this a lack of strength or character on their part. In some cases, people even respond to panic attacks by significantly changing their behavior or situation. This may mean, for example, that they quit their jobs, avoid all physical exertion, or move their residences.

Panic attacks may occur with or without agoraphobia.

PANIC ATTACK WITH AGORAPHOBIA

This multisyllable word is easier to understand if you break it down into two pieces: agora and phobia. In ancient Greece, the "agora" was a large, open place where people could assemble, particularly a marketplace. And according to Webster's dictionary, "phobia" means an irrational, excessive, persistent fear of a thing or a situation. The word "agoraphobia" is formed by combining these two words, and Webster's dictionary defines it as an abnormal fear of being in open or public places.

The essential feature of agoraphobia is an anxiety about being in places or situations from which one might not be able to escape without difficulty or where help might not be available in case of a panic attack (or related symptoms such as dizziness or diarrhea). This fear involves being outside one's home alone and often includes being in crowds, standing in lines, being on a bridge, or traveling in a bus, train, or automobile.

An Assortment of Phobias

- Ablutophobia—fear of washing
- Acrophobia—fear of high places
- Algophobia—fear of pain
- Arithmophobia—fear of arithmetic or numbers
- Bacillophobia—fear of germs
- Cyberphobia—fear of computers or using a computer
- Entomophobia—fear of insects
- Hemophobia—fear of blood
- Nyctophobia—fear of the dark or night
- Pyrophobia—fear of fire
- Technophobia—fear of advanced technology or complex devices
- Venustraphobia—fear of beautiful women
- Xenophobia—fear of strangers
- Zoophobia—fear of animals

Some individuals with agoraphobia venture into such situations but endure intense distress while doing so. Some tolerate such excursions better when they have a companion along, while others find leaving the house all but impossible.

twin studies: Research conducted on twins.

Panic disorder without agoraphobia is diagnosed twice as often in women as in men; with agoraphobia, it is diagnosed three times as often in women. The most typical age of onset of panic disorder is between late adolescence and the mid-30s, although even children and people over age forty-five can experience the onset of this disorder. There appears to be a genetic factor in panic disorder, as indicated by a higher incidence in immediate family members of those with the disorder, and by twin studies.

People with phobias fear many things—spiders, flying, shots, disasters, and enclosed places are just a few examples.

The Phobias

Phobias are intense, persistent fears of specific things or situations. Specific phobia and social phobia are classified as anxiety disorders.

Specific Phobia

This phobia is an excessive or unreasonable fear that a person experiences when in the presence of the feared object or situation, a fear that interferes with the individual's normal functioning. This fear is usually related to the harm the individual anticipates from the object or situation. For instance, many people have phobias about flying in airplanes because they fear what could happen if the airplane crashed, as Trevor Anhalt did in chapter 1. Other people fear dogs (or other animals) because they anticipate the possibility of being bitten or otherwise attacked.

Another type of specific phobia involves fear of losing control, panicking, or fainting in response to blood, injury, heights, elevators, and so on. Several of the specific phobias have become well known by their names (and at least one has been used as a movie title):

- arachnophobia: fear of spiders
- claustrophobia: fear of closed-in spaces
- triskaidekaphobia: fear of the number 13.

Phobia is not diagnosed when an individual experiences a reasonable fear, such as if someone is concerned about being shot when in a dangerous neighborhood or fears a car accident while driving on a crowded, six-lane freeway.

Specific phobia is divided into several subtypes for diagnostic purposes, and the subtypes give an indication of the most common phobias, with the feared objects, places, or situations (known as triggers) in parentheses. Subtypes include:

- animal type (animals or insects)
- natural environment type (storms, heights, water)
- blood-injection-injury type (seeing blood, injury, receiving injections or undergoing other medical procedures)
- situational type (public transportation, tunnels, bridges, elevators, flying, driving, enclosed places)
- other type (choking, vomiting; also includes "space" pho-

A person with social phobia may feel as though everyone is looking at her and laughing.

Someone who has a social phobia may misinterpret social interactions. For instance, she may get upset because she believes people are talking about her behind her back.

bia—fear of falling down if away from walls or other means of support; children's fears of characters in costumes or of loud noises)

Specific phobias may be triggered or contributed to by actual traumatic events, such as choking, being trapped in a closet or other small space, or dog bites. Other contributing factors to specific phobia can include observing people in a traumatic situation and hearing frequent warnings from parents about the dangers of certain objects or situations.

Social Phobia

Social phobia, such as Charlene Williams suffered, is an individual's overwhelming and disabling fear of either social or performance situations where she may be embarrassed or humiliated. Exposure to the feared situation usually provokes an anxiety response, which may take the form of a panic attack. The individual (except in the case of children) realizes that the fear is unreasonable or excessive and is distressed by having it.

inarticulate: Incapable of speech.

For people with social phobia, common responses in social or performance situations may include palpitations, tremors, sweating, gastrointestinal discomfort, diarrhea, muscle tension, blushing, and confusion. The overriding concern seems to be that others will notice that the sufferer's hands or voices tremble in such situations, or that she will appear **inarticulate**, leading other people to consider her weak, crazy, stupid, or anxious. Due to this fear, individuals with social phobia may stop eating, drinking, or writing in public. They will find that their phobia interferes substantially with their functioning at school, work, or other social settings.

Social phobia is the third most common psychiatric disorder in the United States and afflicts about fifteen million people each year. It usually begins in the mid-teens, sometimes in a person who has a childhood history of shyness or of being socially inhibited. At other times it may follow an especially stressful or embarrassing experience, and it can last throughout a person's life, growing more and less prevalent according to his life circumstances. Although community-based studies have found that social phobia is more common in women, clinical samples indicate that both sexes are equally involved or males are in the majority.

Someone who is obsessive-compulsive may check and recheck to make sure he has locked the door.

Obsessive-Compulsive Disorder [OCD]

Obsessive-compulsive disorder is marked by obsessions (persistent ideas, thoughts, impulses, images) and compulsions (usually repetitive behaviors and mental acts). The obsessions can cause severe mental stress, leading to the compulsions, which are usually performed in an attempt to relieve that stress.

The following example is a typical OCD scenario: The individual begins to wonder if he has locked the front door, and the thought occurs over and over in his mind. He goes to the door and checks the lock, but for some reason, the knowledge that the door is locked does not seem to sink in. The thought continues and his stress rises, so he checks the lock again. This pattern may occur over and over so that some people with OCD may check a lock as many as forty to one hundred times in a single evening. The problem is not with the individual's intelligence or memory but with whatever part of the brain that would normally allow him to "know" that the act had been performed.

contamination: Soiled, stained, or infected by contact or association.

Another common OCD scenario involves obsessive thoughts about contamination, perhaps from shaking hands with other people. The stress that results from these recurrent thoughts escalates. In an attempt to alleviate that stress, the individual may begin washing her hands repeatedly. Some people with OCD wash their hands so often—sometimes for hours per day—and so thoroughly that their skin becomes raw and irritated.

The most typical obsessions involve fear of contamination, repeated doubts about whether one has done something (turned off a gas stove, run over someone with a car), a need for things to be ordered or symmetrical, aggressive or horrific impulses (hurting one's child or shouting obscenities in church), or sexual imagery (recurring pornographic images).

Typical compulsions involve hand-washing, putting things in order, checking to make sure something has been done, and mental acts such as praying, counting, and repeating words or phrases.

OCD usually begins in adolescence or early adulthood, although it can also begin in childhood. In adults, OCD is equally common in males and females. When the disorder begins in childhood, however, it is more common in males than in females. When such obsessions and compulsions cause the sufferer significant distress, take

Someone who was kidnapped or experienced some other traumatic event would be at risk of developing posttraumatic stress disorder.

up more than an hour per day, or interfere with an individual's usual activities or relationships, they can be classified as a disorder.

Obsessive-compulsive disorder is a fascinating subject and a discussion of it requires more space than can be allotted in this book. For more information, see *Obsessive-Compulsive Disorder*, another title in this series.

Posttraumatic
Stress Disorder [PTSD]

Posttraumatic stress disorder is different from the other anxiety disorders in that it occurs:

- after experiencing a **traumatic** event that is potentially life threatening or could cause serious, life-threatening injury;
- after witnessing another person face such an event;
- or after learning that a family member or close associate has met an unexpected or violent death, or faced serious harm or the threat of death or injury.

The patient's response involves feelings of intense fear, helplessness, or horror, and his ability to function socially, at school, or at a job is affected negatively. The characteristic symptom of PTSD is a persistent reexperiencing of the traumatic event.

Traumatic events may include military combat, sexual assault, physical attack, robbery, mugging, being kidnapped or taken hostage, a terrorist attack, torture, being made a prisoner of war or kept in a concentration camp, natural and man-made disasters, severe car accidents, and being diagnosed with a life-threatening illness. When the traumatic event is one designed by another human, such as rape or torture, the resulting PTSD may be particularly severe or long lasting.

traumatic: An event that causes mental or emotional stress.

Reexperiencing the traumatic event can include recurring thoughts or dreams about the event and flashbacks (in which the individual actually relives the event and behaves as though experiencing it in the present—a state that is typically brief but may last from a few seconds to days). Events that trigger flashbacks may include anniversaries and circumstances similar to those during which the traumatic event was first experienced. For example, a woman who was raped in an elevator may find entering any elevator to be a **triggering event**.

Commonly, people with PTSD will avoid any stimuli associated with the trauma, including thoughts, feelings, or conversations about it, which may include related activities, situations, or other people. This avoidance may take the form of **amnesia**, either total or partial, or emotional **anesthesia** (also called psychic numbing), which is a lessening of a person's responsiveness to the outside world. This numbing may include decreased interest or participation in things they used to find enjoyable, a feeling of detachment or estrangement from other people, and marked decrease in the ability to feel emotions, particularly those connected with intimacy, tenderness, and sexuality. There may also be sleeping difficulties, irritability, or outbursts of anger.

PTSD can begin at any age. Symptoms usually begin within three months after the trauma, but in some cases they do not show up until months or years later. In about half of PTSD cases, a complete recovery occurs within three months, although many individuals have symptoms for longer than twelve months.

triggering event: Something that causes an emotional or physical response.

amnesia: Partial or total loss of memory.

anesthesia: An absence of feeling—physical or psychological.

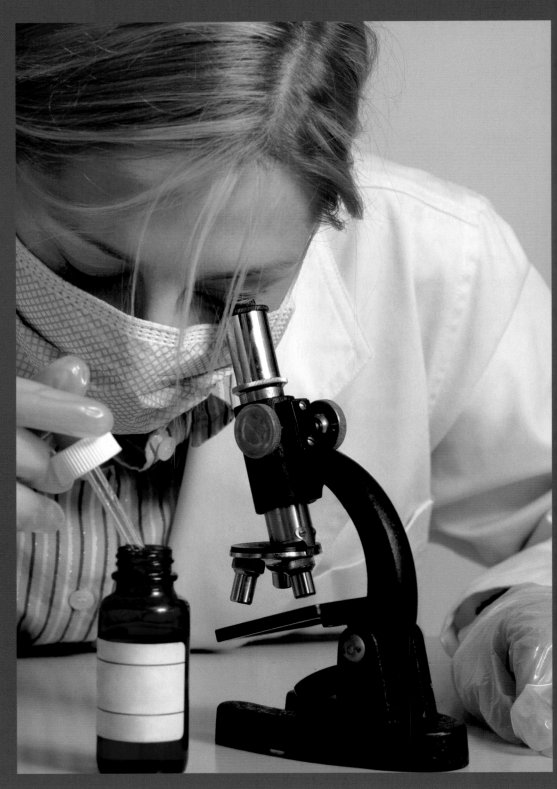

Scientists develop psychiatric drugs through careful research.

Chapter Three

The History of Psychiatric Drugs

assie, Trevor, Charlene, and Tara all eventually took their problems to doctors, who advised them that they were suffering from specific anxiety disorders that required medical treatment. In each case, a drug was prescribed, either to be used alone or in combination with a therapy program (although for one of these patients, the drug was for one-time or infrequent use only). In some of the cases, the doctors explained that practitioners have a choice between several different classes of drugs that can be used to treat anxiety disorders, and each class of drugs had several individual medications from which to choose. But where did these drugs come from—and how were they discovered?

Drugs are discovered and developed in many different ways, and their stories make for interesting reading. Usually researchers are actually studying a particular disease, looking for a way to combat or cure it. The stories behind the development of psychiatric drugs, however, have been quite different from that of other medications. Many psychiatric drugs were discovered almost by accident. Antipsychotic drugs, for example, were discovered for the most part by **anesthesiologists**. When they administered these drugs in order to anesthetize surgical patients, they observed the calming effect the drugs had.

One such example involves Henri Laborit, a surgeon in Paris. In 1952,

anesthesiologists: The doctors who administer the medication that puts surgical patients to sleep or into an altered state of consciousness during surgery.

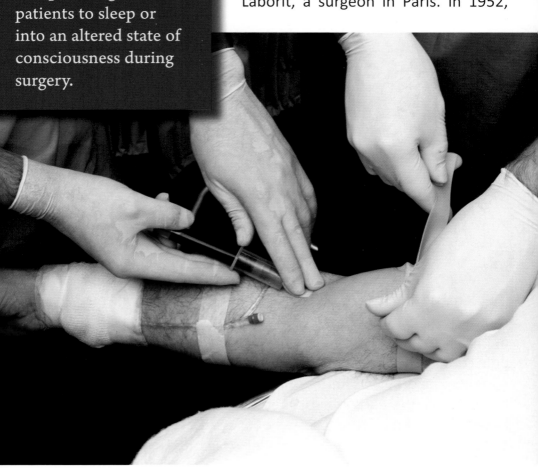

Doctors working to reduce surgical shock stumbled on medications that also treated psychiatric disorders.

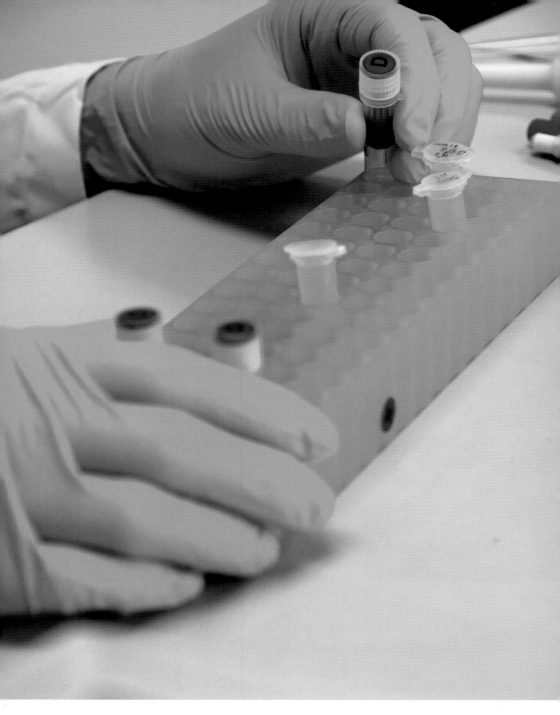

Scientists work in laboratories to predict the effects of various substances on human brain chemicals.

Drug Discoveries That Changed the World

When Sir Alexander Fleming (1881–1955), a doctor and research bacteriologist at St. Mary's Hospital in London, England, was serving in World War I, he was deeply saddened and distressed by the large number of soldiers who died from bacterial infection of their wounds. As a result, he determined to study bacteria after the war ended. One day in 1928, he noticed mold growing in one of his laboratory cultures and began to observe the culture carefully. He saw that wherever the mold grew, the bacteria were destroyed. He studied and experimented with the mold, and eventually, after many years of research, a powerful antibiotic with great lifesaving potential was developed. The mold was a species of Penicillium, so Sir Fleming named it penicillin, a name now familiar to millions of people around the world.

For other diseases, such as poliomyelitis (polio), antibiotics were not effective. As late as the 1950s, polio was still a dreaded illness that frequently crippled or paralyzed young people. Then Jonas Edward Salk (1914–1995), associate professor of bacteriology and head of the Virus Research Laboratory at the University of Pittsburgh School of Medicine, began research on a polio vaccine and eventually developed a vaccine that was effective against all three viruses that cause polio.

Laborit was puzzling over a way to reduce surgical shock in his patients, caused for the most part by anesthesia. He felt that if he could use less anesthetic during surgery, his patients could recover more quickly. Since shock was known to result from certain brain chemicals, he decided to try using another chemical to counteract this effect. He tried antihistamines, drugs that are usually used to fight allergies.

Laborit noticed that when he gave his patients a strong dose of antihistamines, they no longer seemed anxious about their upcoming surgery. As a result, Laborit could use much less anesthetic during the operation. The physical effect of the antihistamines was even more far-reaching than what Laborit originally intended, affecting his patients' mental state so strongly that the doctor began to think these drugs—especially chlorpromazine hydrochloride—might be of some use in the field of psychiatry.

The climate in psychiatry at that time, however, dictated that electric shock or various psychotherapies were the treatments of choice. "No one in his right mind in psychiatry was working with drugs," Canadian psychiatrist Heinz Lehmann says of that period. But one colleague of Laborit's told his brother-in-law, psychiatrist

In the early twentieth century, most people with psychiatric disorders were placed in hospitals like this one.

A person with schizophrenia may have bizarre hallucinations.

Pierre Deniker, what had happened with the chlorpromazine. Deniker ordered some of the drug to try on his most agitated, uncontrollable patients.

Deniker was amazed by the results. Patients who had been restrained because of their violent behavior and patients who "had stood in one spot without moving for weeks" could now be left without supervision and could actually respond to other people.

Severe mental illness had been growing in America between the years of 1904, when two out of a thousand people were institutionalized in mental hospitals, and 1955, when the number had risen to four out of a thousand. There was really nothing available to help the mentally ill, and they were routinely "warehoused" in state institutions. At the same time, an American drug company named Smith-Kline was hoping to expand its line of drugs. SmithKline heard about chlorpromazine, bought the rights to it from a European company called Rhone-Poulenc, and then marketed it in the United States as an anti-vomiting medication. SmithKline tried to convince American medical schools and university psychology departments to test the drug for psychiatric use, but chlorpromazine was considered just another sedative. Academics and doctors were still interested in treating mental disorders solely with **psychoanalysis** and **behaviorism**.

SmithKline then asked Dr. Deniker to help influence doctors in America to use the drug, and he did so. The first successes for chlorpromazine came in state institutions, where test results seemed miraculous. When chlorpromazine was approved by the U.S. Food and Drug Administration in 1954, it had a huge effect on thousands, even millions, of people with mental disorders. It decreased the intensity of **schizophrenia** symptoms such as hallucinations and delusions. It calmed people without sedating

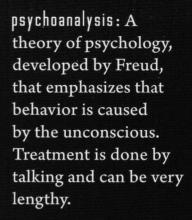

psychoanalysis: A theory of psychology, developed by Freud, that emphasizes that behavior is caused by the unconscious. Treatment is done by talking and can be very lengthy.

behaviorism: An approach to psychology that believes that all psychological responses can be traced to physical causes that can be directly observed.

schizophrenia: A psychotic disorder characterized by a loss of contact with reality. Symptoms can include auditory and visual hallucinations and disorganized speech patterns.

Medication provided psychiatric patients with new treatment options.

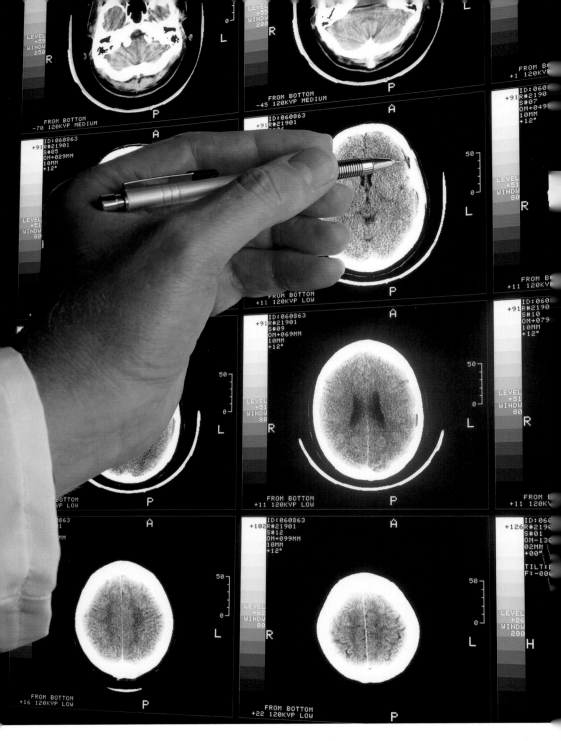

MRIs provide detailed images of the brain.

them and, in many cases, allowed them to lead an almost normal life. By 1964, fifty million people around the world had taken the drug, and SmithKline had doubled their revenues three times.

Although side effects and other drawbacks associated with chlorpromazine eventually came to light, the dramatic effects this chemical had on the brain led people to think differently about brain function and behavior.

For instance, symptoms similar to those of Parkinson's disease were side effects of chlorpromazine, which made researchers begin considering the possibility that similar chemicals might be involved in natural Parkinson's disease—and could be counteracted. This type of thinking eventually resulted in understanding the role of dopamine and other neurotransmitters, an advance that has had a great impact on the treatment of mental disorders. (See chapter four for an explanation of how neurotransmitters work in the central nervous system.)

After chlorpromazine, drug companies went on to develop and market other medicines to treat psychiatric problems. The benzodiazepines (such as Valium and Xanax) decreased anxiety but could also produce troublesome side effects. Researchers developed many drugs for the treatment of depression, including Tofranil and Elavil in the 1960s, and Prozac, Zoloft, and Paxil in the 1980s.

Next, the antipsychotic drugs were observed to relieve psychotic symptoms such as hallucinations and delusions, which are common in patients with schizophrenia. When the discovery was made that the antipsychotic drugs block dopamine receptors in the brain, scientists began to wonder if schizophrenia, or any part of it, could be a result of an excess of dopamine. After that, scientists questioned whether depression could be related to a lack of the neurotransmitters serotonin and noradrenaline, and if anxiety could be caused by a lack of GABA (a neurotransmitter called gamma-aminobutyric acid).

In order to develop new drugs that affect the brain, scientists know they need a better understanding of how the brain works. While it is relatively simple to tell what is going on in other body organs by means of a blood test, information about the brain is not so easily accessible. Because of what scientists refer to as the blood–brain barrier, many medicines are not able to get into the brain. Now, however, the following valuable methods for "seeing" the living, intact brain have been developed:

- CAT (computerized axial tomography) scans: reveals brain structures without harming the patient.
- MRI (magnetic resonance imaging): gives highly refined pictures of the brain using magnetic fields and without using radiation.
- PET (positron emission tomography) and SPECT (single-pho-

The blood–brain barrier keeps some medicines out of the brain.

ton emission computed tomography): reveal brain structure and also show metabolic activity in various parts of the brain (brain chemicals and their receptors).

With the development of these last tests, scientists can now inject chemicals labeled with tiny amounts of radioactivity into a person's bloodstream and watch where in the brain they go and to what they bind. These imaging techniques are used to see abnormalities in the brains of people with panic disorder, depression, obsessive-compulsive disorder, and schizophrenia and are helping scientists learn more about the receptors for antipsychotic and benzodiazepine antianxiety drugs.

Research continues on other fronts, as well. With the advent of genetic research, molecular geneticists have linked some psychiatric diseases, such as schizophrenia and bipolar disorder, to abnormal genes. Other researchers have developed methods to study psychotherapies under controlled conditions. This means that psychotherapies and drug therapies can now be compared scientifically so that practitioners will soon have a better understanding of the uses and the limitations of both types of treatment.

bipolar disorder: A psychological disorder characterized by periods of extreme highs alternating with extreme lows.

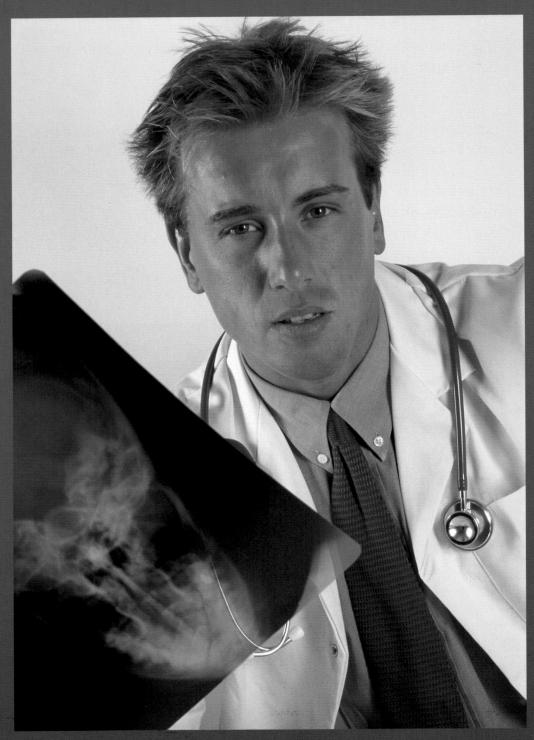

Using a variety of tests and diagnostic procedures, doctors and advanced practice nurses determine the best treatment plan for patients with anxiety disorders.

Chapter Four

Treatment Descriptions

I f you are feeling so sick that you cannot function at school, you will probably go to a doctor. The doctor will diagnose your illness and then write a prescription; often your treatment will involve taking a specific drug or medication that will help you to feel better. In a similar way, when a person is diagnosed with an anxiety disorder, the psychiatrist (a doctor specially trained to treat the mind) will often prescribe a drug that will help the patient to better cope with her life.

Cassie McCauley

When Cassie's parents went with her to the psychiatrist's office, Cassie was embarrassed to describe the symptoms she had been experiencing in front of them. She worried that her parents would think she was crazy. Instead, they affirmed how much they loved and valued her, and how much they wanted to see that she get whatever treatment was necessary to restore her to full health.

Cassie felt both exhausted and elated—exhausted at the emotional strain of finally admitting the truth to other people but elated because she had done just that, and the others weren't acting as though they thought she were crazy or worthless. Did that mean this strange thing she was going through could be treated? Deep inside, Cassie felt a flicker of hope. Perhaps there was a way out of this terrible problem. After a complete physical and psychiatric exam, the psychiatrist explained that Cassie, along with about three percent of the population, had panic disorder.

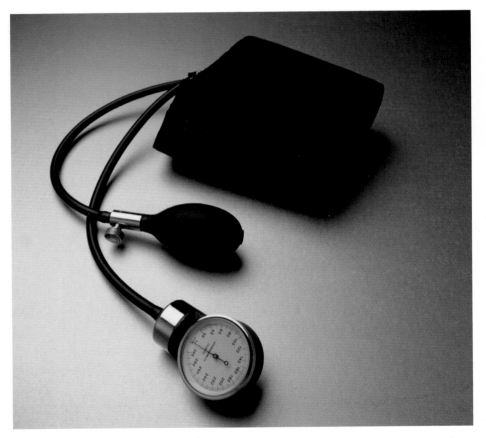

Blood pressure should be monitored when a person is taking some psychiatric medications.

Little Albert

The Little Albert study, conducted in 1920 by John B. Watson, founder of the behaviorist school, conditioned a nine-month-old infant named Albert to fear a white rat by scaring him with a loud noise each time he was in the rat's presence. Since Albert was not afraid of the rat prior to his conditioning, Watson concluded that phobias and various other emotional disturbances could also be learned in this same way.

"You'll be glad to know that panic disorder responds very well to a number of psychiatric drugs on the market. The cyclic antidepressants, such as imipramine, were the first drugs we had to treat panic disorder," the psychiatrist explained. "They work well, but you have low blood pressure, a problem imipramine might worsen. So I think I'll start you out on a very low dose of fluoxetine hydrochloride—you've probably heard of it as Prozac—one of a class of drugs known as SSRIs, or selective serotonin reuptake inhibitors. We'll start with 10 milligrams per day and work our way up from there. Now let me warn you, Cassie. . ." The psychiatrist leaned forward to emphasize her point. "This medication can take a while to work. You may notice some side effects within a few days, but it won't make a change in these panic attack symptoms for at least two to four weeks. So in the meantime, while you're waiting, I'm going to prescribe another drug called Ativan. I don't want you taking this drug for more than a few weeks, because it can be addictive—but it will take effect right away. Once the Prozac is working, we'll stop the Ativan. We're also going to talk every week, and I'll make sure your principal and teachers know exactly what's going on."

When she first went on the medicine, Cassie noticed she began to feel slightly nauseated and noticed a decrease in her appetite. She called the doctor, and together they agreed that the side effects were slight enough that Cassie could put up with them. At school,

Cassie's principal and teachers agreed to help as much as they could during this trial of the drug.

"If you feel one of these attacks starting, you just let us know immediately, and you can go to the nurse's office until you feel better," they told her. Just knowing that she had their support helped lessen Cassie's anticipatory anxiety of more panic attacks.

As Cassie no longer experienced panic attacks, eventually, she forgot to think about her panic disorder all the time. She found herself more and more involved in her schoolwork and social activities, the way she had been before September 11. As the panic attacks lessened, both in frequency and intensity, Cassie gradually began trusting herself to go shopping with her mother again. She also gained the courage to call Brian and explain why she had been avoiding him. He was skeptical at first, but after he read some of the information the psychiatrist had given her, he became Cassie's strongest supporter in her efforts to fully recover.

Cassie stayed on the medication for nearly eight months, then she began to taper off of it very gradually. She also began the program of cognitive/behavioral therapy her psychiatrist suggested. The panic attacks eventually became only an unpleasant memory, but if they ever returned, Cassie knew now how to combat them.

anticipatory anxiety: Anxiety caused by the worrying between panic attacks about the next attack.

cognitive/behavioral therapy: A short-term therapy focused on specific symptoms. The patient is taught to recognize what causes those symptoms and to redirect his or her thinking and patterns of behavior to avoid those symptoms.

Trevor Anhalt

Trevor's first visit to the therapist was a disappointment. He'd heard there were many drugs available for the kind of problem he had and had made up his mind that medication was the way he wanted to go.

"I have a different idea," said the therapist. "Let me explain." He described a treatment plan consisting of cognitive/behavioral therapy that would gradually expose Trevor to airplanes, lessening his fear over a period of time.

"But I heard on TV that there are all these drugs you can take if you're anxious. . ." Trevor protested.

"However, those drugs are not meant for specific phobias, which is what you're dealing with," the therapist answered. "Think about it, Trevor. Would you want to take a psychiatric drug every day for the long term when you may only face flying once in a great while? That's not to say that I won't prescribe a short-term drug, one of the benzodiazepines for instance, for you to take when you actually have to fly. I'll help you any way I can. But therapy will be of more use to you in the long run for this particular disorder."

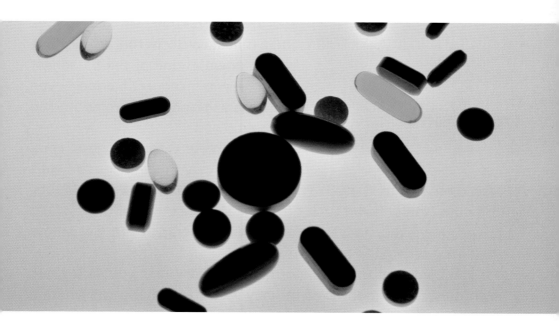

Medication can offer hope and practical help to someone with a phobia.

Trevor really hadn't planned on doing anything so time-consuming as going through a therapy program, but his family strongly encouraged him to do so and promised to support him through it. "We really want to take this trip, Trevor. It would be a great experience for our family. But your health is far more important than any trip, and even if we never go to Hawaii together, you need to deal with this problem."

Trevor entered therapy. He also had the therapist explain to the soda company why he hadn't been able to take the trip he'd been awarded. When officials there heard the real reason, they told Trevor they would extend the trip deadline for as long as he needed to conquer his fear of flying.

Trevor went through all the therapy sessions, which involved **exposure** and **desensitization**. On the day he could finally walk inside an airplane and sit down in one of the passenger seats he was filled with pride—even though the plane was simply parked on the runway.

Once Trevor's therapy was complete, his family made plans to finally take their trip to Hawaii. Privately, Trevor still had a few doubts. "How do I know I won't start freaking out once that airplane starts to taxi down the runway?" he asked his therapist the day before they were scheduled to depart.

"I'm confident that you'll remember everything you've learned in these last few months of therapy. And this is the point where a medication may be useful," the therapist told Trevor. "Klonopin, one of the benzodiazepines, can start to work in under an hour. I'll prescribe just enough to help you with the flights over and back. You

exposure: Being presented to something or someone, often something anxiety provoking.

desensitization: A behavioral treatment method of easing a patient's fears by systematically introducing the anxiety-provoking stimuli to the patient in ever increasing numbers or frequency.

Brand Names vs. Generic Names

Talking about psychiatric drugs can be confusing, because every drug has at least two names: its "generic name" and the "brand name" that the pharmaceutical company uses to market the drug. Generic names come from the drugs' chemical structures, while brand names are used by drug companies in order to inspire public recognition and loyalty for their products.

Here are the brand names and generic names for some common psychiatric drugs used to treat anxiety disorders:

- Ativan® • lorazepam
- Effexor® • venlafaxine
- Elavil® • amitriptyline
- Inderal® • propranolol
- Klonopin® • clonazepam
- Librium® • chlordiazepoxide
- Luvox® • fluvoxamine
- Marplan® • isocarboxazid
- Norpramin® • desipramine
- Paxil® • paroxetine
- Prozac® • fluoxetine
- Tofranil® • imipramine hydrochloride
- Valium® • diazepam
- Xanax® • alprazolam
- Zoloft® • sertraline hydrochloride

What are the signs I may need a psychiatric drug?

1. Feelings of depression, anxiety, or panic for no obvious reason.
2. Difficulty doing your usual work because of depression or anxiety.
3. You can't stop worrying, even though friends or family tell you things are not as bad as you think.
4. People tell you you're "not yourself."
5. You begin to drink more, take over-the-counter drugs, or even borrow prescription medicines from family or friends to help you sleep or make you feel calmer.
6. You begin to feel life simply isn't worth living or begin to think about suicide.
7. You act in strange ways or in ways that frighten others.

Adapted from *The Essential Guide to Psychiatric Drugs*, by Jack M. Gorman.

put the medicine in your carry-on bag, and that way, you'll know you have help available if you absolutely need it."

"Why didn't we use this drug before and save me all that time I spent on therapy?" Trevor joked, but the therapist's answer was serious.

"Because Klonopin is habit forming, both physically and psychologically. It can also affect your memory and your muscle coordination, so you wouldn't want to use it in other situations, say, if you had to drive a car or operate heavy equipment."

Just knowing that he had the Klonopin in his carry-on bag helped Trevor get through the flight without using it. Today, Trevor is a phar-

A person with a social phobia or social anxiety disorder may become so fearful that she withdraws from everyone around her.

maceutical salesman whose job requires him to fly several times a year; he does so without experiencing terror.

Charlene Williams

Charlene quit going to any social occasions, and before long, she rarely even spoke to her closest friends. Her parents were deeply

Drug Approval

Before a drug can be marketed in the United States, it must be officially approved by the Food and Drug Administration (FDA). Today's FDA is the primary consumer protection agency in the United States. Operating under the authority given it by the government, and guided by laws established throughout the twentieth century, the FDA has established a rigorous drug approval process that verifies the safety, effectiveness, and accuracy of labeling for any drug marketed in the United States.

While the United States has the FDA for the approval and regulation of drugs and medical devices, Canada has a similar organization called the Therapeutic Product Directorate (TPD). The TPD is a division of Health Canada, the Canadian government department of health. The TPD regulates drugs, medical devices, disinfectants, and sanitizers with disinfectant claims. Some of the things that the TPD monitors are quality, effectiveness, and safety. Just as the FDA must approve new drugs in the United States, the TPD must approve new drugs in Canada before those drugs can enter the market.

concerned and finally took her to a psychiatrist, Dr. Brewerton, who specialized in anxiety disorders.

Dr. Brewerton listened carefully as Charlene told him all that had happened; he took notes as she spoke and nodded encouragingly. When Charlene finished, the doctor said gently, "I only wish you'd come to see me sooner. I think I could have saved you a lot of pain."

"But what's wrong with me?" Charlene asked. "I've never been like this. I'm turning into a—a hermit!"

"Would you believe me if I told you that about fifteen million Americans have the same problem you do? It's known by two names—social anxiety disorder (SAD) and social phobia. After depression and alcoholism, it's the third most common type of psychological disorder."

Charlene sat back in her chair and stared at the doctor, trying to take it all in. "Ten million people have this? And I've never even heard of it?"

"That's right, and it's important that you get treatment because it often precedes alcoholism, panic disorder, or depression."

"So what do I do?" Charlene asked.

"Well, if you had social phobia related to only one trigger situation—such as speaking in public or performing musically—then we could give you a drug like a simple beta-blocker; Tenormin (the brand name for atenolol), for instance. That type of drug can help people get through a specific stressful situation. But from what you're telling me, your problem is broader than that. It appears that you're going to need a drug that will be taken every day for an extended period of time, so I think we'll start out with Paxil." Dr. Brewerton went on to explain that Paxil (paroxetine hydrochloride, one of the SSRIs), was the first drug to be officially approved in the United States (in 1999) for the treatment of social phobia.

"We'll start you off with twenty milligrams a day, then increase the dose a little each week up to maybe fifty or sixty milligrams. You may notice a few side effects right away, but it will take two to four weeks after we reach the higher dose before the medication actually affects the SAD."

Charlene was excited at the thought that help was available. She started the Paxil that day and never missed a dose. She found some of the side effects of Paxil disturbing, however. She began gaining weight, no matter how drastically she cut back on carbohydrates and fats.

"In some ways, I feel a lot better," Charlene told Dr. Brewerton after six weeks on the Paxil. "I'm much less anxious around people, and I've even started going out with some of my friends again. But I'm eleven pounds heavier now, and that's certainly not helping me feel better about myself! Do I have any other choices?"

Dr. Brewerton nodded. "Let's try venlafaxine, which you may have heard of as Effexor XR."

On venlafaxine, Charlene did so well she was eventually able to return to her normal school and social schedule, and only rarely did she struggle with bothersome thoughts that people were judging her negatively.

Tara Rogers

Tara's treatment also involved Effexor XR, one of the newest antidepressants to be approved for the treatment of Generalized Anxiety Disorder (GAD). Within a few weeks after beginning drug treatment, Tara was enjoying her new position at work instead of worrying constantly that she would be found incompetent.

Diagnosing Anxiety Disorders

Effective treatment always starts with correct diagnosis, so a doctor will first rule out possible biological causes for anxiety. Medical conditions that can cause anxiety-like symptoms include thyroid disorders, hypoglycemia, Cushing's disease, and pheochromocytoma (a tumor of the adrenal gland). Medications such as theophylline preparations for asthma and decongestants such as pseudoephedrine and phenylephrine can also cause anxiety. Caffeine, which is found in coffee, tea, soda, and chocolate, frequently makes anxiety worse, as was mentioned in chapter one. Although alcohol and nicotine (in tobacco) may initially relax users, both substances increase anxiety in the long run.

Treatment Decisions

After causes such as those listed above are ruled out and the presence of an anxiety disorder is diagnosed, doctors must decide between the treatments available. The treatment of disorders such as the ones described in this book arise from theories about the etiology of the disorders themselves.

> etiology: The cause or origin of a disease.

Although many smokers have a cigarette to relax, nicotine can actually raise anxiety levels.

At one time, anxiety was viewed as a signal of a person's defenses against uncomfortable memories and feelings. This theory was based on the pioneering work of Sigmund Freud (1856–1939), the Austrian founder of psychoanalysis. According to Richard S. Perrotto and Joseph Culkin in Exploring Abnormal Psychology, a "Freudian analyst interprets a feared stimulus as an external, symbolic representation of the repressed wish . . . (and) believed that an agoraphobic woman's fear of venturing alone in public symbolically represented her unconscious wish to be seduced." According to this system of thought, anxiety was be-

maladaptive: Not leading to proper adjustment.

relaxation training:
The teaching of such practices as meditation, yoga, and guided imagery that may relax the patient and alleviate some symptoms of anxiety.

biofeedback: The use of instruments to provide information about such physiological processes as blood pressure, muscle tension, and brainwave activity, that are not usually perceived. The patient can sometimes learn to control these processes through relaxation techniques.

lieved to really be a signal of deeper emotional conflict.

Psychodynamic theory recognizes other factors, including problems in interpersonal relationships, that may be involved in the development of anxiety disorders. Behaviorists attribute anxiety disorders to **maladaptive** learning, based on conditioned emotional responses such as the one researchers were able to produce in a research subject named Little Albert (see sidebar p. 61). Behavioral and cognitive therapies would recommend the use of stress-management techniques, **relaxation training**, and **biofeedback** techniques to combat anxiety disorders.

The chemical imbalance theory of anxiety disorders comes from the biological model of the mind, a way of looking at the mind that suggests psychiatric disorders result from abnormalities in the brain's biological makeup.

All these models, however, fail to provide the entire answer for where anxiety disorders originate and how to treat them. According to Dr. Edward Drummond in his book *The Complete Guide to Psychiatric Drugs*, the biopsychosocial model is a more accurate model for understanding and treating psychiatric disorders. It recognizes the three main areas of our life that can interact to produce psychological problems:

- biology (including our genes, brain chemistry, medical conditions and drugs);

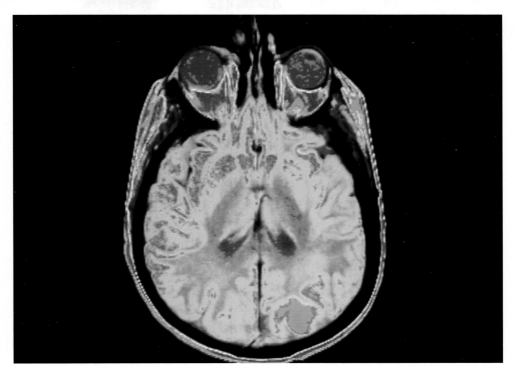

According to the chemical imbalance theory, anxiety disorders result from chemical or structural abnormalities within the brain. Although MRIs provide researchers with detailed images, scientists cannot yet look at an image like the one above to diagnose an anxiety disorder.

- psychology (our feelings, desires, thoughts, and behaviors); and
- social experience (events and people).

Medical practitioners must take into account the many different treatments now available to help people with psychiatric disorders and then prescribe the ones most suited to the patient and the situation. Treatment with psychiatric drugs may include a number of options, depending on the specific disorder and the patient's individual needs.

Generalized
Anxiety Disorder [GAD]

Generalized anxiety disorder is usually treated best with selective serotonin reuptake inhibitors (SSRIs) and tricyclic antidepressants (TCAs).

SSRIs must be taken every day and need some weeks before they become effective. Drugs in this group include (but are not limited to) Prozac (fluoxetine), Luvox (fluvoxamine maleate), Paxil (paroxetine hydrochloride), and Zoloft (sertraline hydrochloride). When a patient first starts taking one of these medications, her anxiety may actually get worse before it starts to improve. To avoid this, medical practitioners often start with low doses and increase them slowly until the patient begins to experience improvement. These medications can be helpful with depression as well, so they are a good choice if the patient is suffering from both anxiety and depression.

TCAs are considered the second or third choice of drugs for treating anxiety. If a person has attention-deficit/hyperactivity disorder as well as anxiety, TCAs are a good choice, since they can treat both disorders simultaneously. TCAs also must be taken every day and need some weeks before they become effective. Drugs in this group include (but are not limited to) Elavil (amitriptyline), clomipramine, imipramine, Norpramin (desipramine), and Surmontil (trimipramine maleate).

Benzodiazepines are also used in the treatment of GAD. They offer faster initial relief because they can become effective within a much shorter period of time (thirty to sixty minutes), but they can become habit forming with long-term use. They can also become ineffective over time and cause a rebound in symptoms if stopped abruptly or tapered off. Benzodiazepines include (but are not limited to) Valium (diazepam), Ativan (lorazepam), Xanax (alprazolam), and Librium (chlordiazepoxide). Benzodiazepines are often prescribed on a short-term basis while an SSRI or TCA is being gradually increased.

Buspirone and trazodone hydrochloride are also sometimes used in treating GAD.

Benzodiazepines provide quick relief for anxiety disorders.

Panic Disorder

When patients need very quick relief from panic attacks, benzodiazepines can help because of the speed with which they become effective. However, because they are habit forming, they should be used only for short-term treatment. Extended treatment can be done with SSRIs and TCAs, which will take some weeks to work effectively but can provide long-term relief from daily anxiety. MAOIs (monoamine oxidase inhibitors) such as Nardil (phenelzine sulfate), Marplan (isocarboxazid), and Eldepryl (selegiline HCl) can offer effective long-term treatment of panic disorders, but their possible side effects (which, among other things, require patients to adhere to a very strict diet) make them troublesome for most patients.

The Phobias [Social and Specific]

In most cases, social phobia responds well to SSRIs and TCAs. For social phobia that is triggered by specific occasions (performance events, etc.), some patients cope well with only a beta-blocker, such as Tenormin (atenolol) or Inderal (propranolol HCl), taken an hour or so before the event. Beta-blockers are not effective for social phobia when taken on a daily basis.

Specific phobia of single triggers (a fear of dogs or airplanes, for example) responds better to therapy than to drugs, because the patient is usually not around the object he fears enough to warrant ongoing, daily drug doses.

Obsessive-Compulsive Disorder [OCD]

SSRIs such as Luvox (fluvoxamine) and TCAs such as clomipramine generally prove effective. Anafranil, Luvox, and Zoloft have been approved by the FDA to treat OCD. However, research indicates that other SSRIs may also be effective treatment for this disorder, although higher doses of SSRIs may be needed when treating OCD. Other classes of drugs are usually ineffective for OCD. Behavioral treatment is the only effective form of psychotherapy used for OCD, and it is usually supplemented by medication. (For more information, see *Obsessive-Compulsive Disorder* in this series.)

Posttraumatic Stress Disorder [PTSD]

SSRIs can help lessen the intensity of anxiety and flashbacks and can also help a patient to sleep better. While the benzodiazepines can provide quick help, they are habit forming, and their effectiveness wears off with long-term use. TCAs and MAOIs are helpful but have more side effects.

Psychiatric drugs can provide amazing help for people suffering from a psychiatric disorder. But they are not magic pills that automati-

A person with posttraumatic stress disorder will mentally and emotionally relive past trauma.

cally cure every problem. Some patients may also need to make life-style changes (including diet, exercise, constructive activities, and learning to build healthy relationships). For others, their doctor's prescription may include psychotherapy as well as one of the many medicines now available to treat anxiety disorders. (Therapies and other remedies will be mentioned in chapter seven, "Alternative and Supplementary Treatments.") Some patients will be treated with a combination of all these options. Psychiatric disorders can cause a person great pain—but treatment offers hope.

Many psychiatric medications need to be taken at the same time each day in order for them to work effectively.

Chapter Five

How Does the Drug Work?

After Cassie spent a few weeks regularly taking Prozac, she was beginning to function well again, as a daughter and a friend. Although she became very familiar with the positive results of this medication, she wasn't aware of what was going on inside her head, where the medicine was blocking the reuptake of serotonin by the presynaptic neurons.

Trevor still carries a prescription for Klonopin, just in case he ever needs it. If he had taken it, it would have intensified the effect of GABA. GABA is an inhibitory neurotransmitter that is released by the presynaptic neuron. All the benzodiazepine antianxiety drugs, including well-known ones such as Valium and Xanax, increase the activity of GABA, which in turn reduces neurons' transmissions of impulses. This reduces anxiety and also makes people feel sleepy.

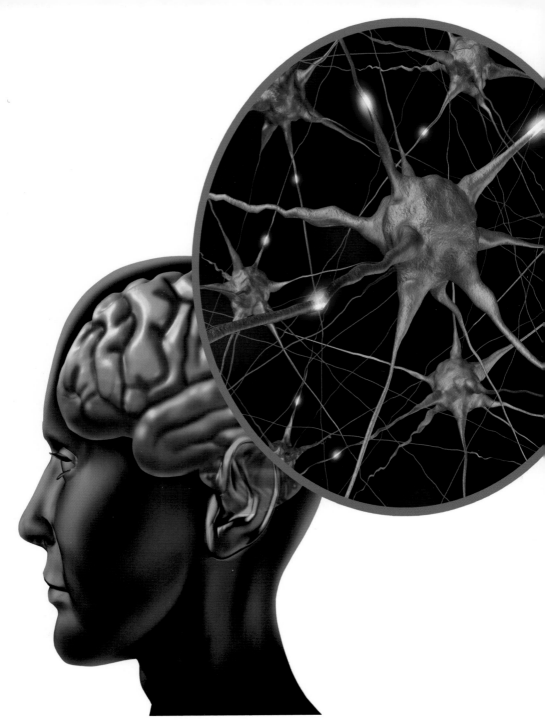

The human brain takes in messages from and sends messages out to the entire body.

Charlene tried Paxil first, which blocks the reuptake of serotonin of presynaptic neurons, but found the side effects too unpleasant. Effexor XR, an antidepressant and the drug that helped both Charlene and Tara, works by blocking the reuptake of both norepinephrine and serotonin into pre-synaptic neurons.

If Dr. Brewerton had prescribed a beta-blocker, such as atenolol, for Charlene, that drug would have blocked adrenaline, a hormone produced by the adrenal gland, which stimulates body organs such as the heart and sweat glands. When these drugs block symptoms of anxiety (a racing heart, for instance, or sweating), the patient often feels more confident to perform or speak in a social situation.

If Charlene had not been helped by either Paxil or Effexor XR, her doctor might have tried Nardil (phenelzine), one of the MAOIs. This class of drugs works by inhibiting a protein enzyme (monoamine oxidase), which breaks down neurotransmitters such as dopamine, epinephrine, norepinephrine, and serotonin. This results in a higher level of those transmitters. The MAOIs, however, can be difficult drugs to use, since they cannot be combined with a long list of other medicines and foods, resulting in a very strict diet for patients.

Psychiatric drugs such as Prozac and the others mentioned have specific effects on body cells and chemicals. In order to comprehend how these drugs operate, it is important to first understand a little about how the brain works.

Inside the Human Brain

The sheer complexity of the human brain is amazing. Inside it are millions and millions of neurons—specialized brain cells that are capable of passing on messages to other neurons. There are so many neurons in our brains that if all the neurons and their axons from a single human brain were stretched end to end, they would reach to the moon and back.

But the cells within the brain do not operate alone. The brain is part of the central nervous system (CNS), which also includes the spinal cord. Between the brain and the CNS, each individual has bil-

Dr. Jack M. Gorman, in *The New Psychiatry*, stresses the importance of a patient's knowing whether or not the prescribed medication is working. "The one advantage of medication over other forms of psychiatric treatment is that an effect is usually discernible in a matter of weeks; no one should ever continue to take medication unless it is clear there is a benefit," he says. The drugs' effect—usually quite concrete—is to relieve and often eliminate specific symptoms. For those with panic disorder, these specific symptoms include panic attacks, anticipatory anxiety, and phobias; for those with generalized anxiety disorder, the specific symptom would be a high anxiety level; for those with social phobia, anxiety attacks during social and performance situations.

In order to not expect more from a drug than it can do, he encourages patients to realize that psychiatric drugs cannot:

- improve one's basic personality;
- give one job success or a better marriage;
- make one smarter, more athletic, or a better parent.

However, psychiatric drugs can free a person from anxiety symptoms to the point that she can participate in other forms of therapy and begin to cope with other problems in her life.

lions of neurons, both sensory and motor. Our five senses—sight, hearing, smell, touch, and taste—feed information from the outside world to the brain by way of the sensory neurons. Motor neurons respond to this information by making the muscles of our bodies move.

How does this vast communication system work in real life? Let's say that Duncan, who is too young to understand the dangers of fire, is roasting marshmallows by threading them onto a long stick, then holding that stick over an open campfire. In a hurry to get to the good part (eating a nicely browned, gooey marshmallow), Duncan inches closer and closer to the fire so his stick can reach the hottest part of the flames. Unfortunately, he gets a bit too close. When a flame flares up suddenly, it makes unexpected contact with Duncan's little finger, stimulating a nerve cell there.

In a flash, the nerve cell in Duncan's finger conducts a message along its axons to the spinal cord. There, information is relayed to other neurons, which send information back to Duncan's hand, telling it to move. Fast.

However, that's not the end of the message relay going on just then inside Duncan's body. If Duncan doesn't learn from this experience that fire can hurt, his little finger could face the same kind of danger again in the future. So the information that fire is hot—and

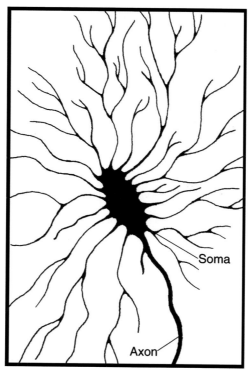

A nerve cell.

that he should keep his hand away from it—is relayed to yet other neurons, and this important information is stored in Duncan's memory.

How do messages, or neural impulses, travel through the body to the spine or brain? Much of the answer lies in the structure of the neuron itself. In one area of the neuron, the cell body sends out dendrites, projections that look like tiny twigs. In another area of the neuron, the cell body extends a long thin filament called an axon. At the end of the axon are several terminal buttons. The terminal buttons lie on the dendrites of another neuron so that each neuron functions as a link in the communication chain. The chain does not run in just one direction, however. Because each neuron is in contact with many other neurons, the CNS is like a vast mesh or web of interconnected groups of neurons. The communication connections and interconnections possible between these millions of neurons, with their cell bodies, axons, and dendrites, is an amazing thing to consider.

A bipolar neuron (one with two sets of dendrites).

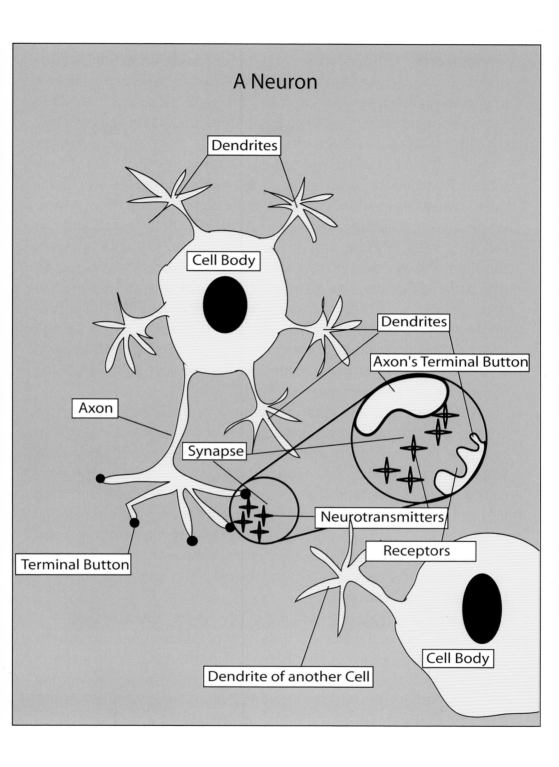

A Neuron

Brain cells communicate by sending electrical signals from neuron to neuron. Although axons and dendrites do not actually touch other neurons, they lie very close together. In between cells is a tiny space called a synapse, and it is through this space that nerve impulses travel, jumping the space in much the same way an electric current would. When a message is to be transferred, a neuron "fires," and its terminal buttons release chemicals called neurotransmitters (biochemical substances such as norepinephrine and dopamine), which make it possible for the message to jump the synapse. When an electrical signal comes to the end of one neuron and the cell fires, secreting the proper neurotransmitter into the synapse, this chemical messenger then crosses from the presynaptic neuron (the brain cell sending the message) to the postsynaptic neuron (the brain cell receiving the message), where it binds itself to the appropriate chemical receptor and influences the behavior of this second neuron. Neurotransmitters can influence the behavior of the postsynaptic neuron by either transmitting the message or by inhibiting the passage of the message.

When a neurotransmitter binds to receptors, other processes are set in motion in the postsynaptic brain cell, either exciting it to continue transmission of the electrical impulse or inhibiting it to stop the transmission. After the impulse is passed from one neuron to another, the neurotransmitter falls off the receptor and back into the synapse, where it is either taken back into the presynaptic neuron (a kind of neuron recycling), broken down by enzymes, and discarded to spinal fluid surrounding the brain—or reattaches itself to the receptor, thus strengthening the original signal traveling from the presynaptic neuron.

Amazingly, at least one hundred billion synapses exist in the brain. Researchers presently know of about thirty different neurotransmitters, but new ones are being discovered all the time. Some experts speculate that there may be hundreds. And many neurons respond to more than one neurotransmitter. Psychiatric drugs operate in this complex environment of the brain, usually exerting their effects on neurotransmitters. The operations of these drugs are also complex, but it can be said that their main function is to make the postsynaptic neuron either more or less likely to fire.

Different classes of drugs operate in different ways. The drugs commonly used to treat anxiety disorders fall into the following categories:

- benzodiazepines (examples: Xanax, Ativan, Valium, Tranxene, Klonopin)
- selective serotonin reuptake inhibitors (SSRIs; examples: Prozac, Zoloft, Paxil, Celexa, Luvox)
- tricyclic antidepressants (TCAs; examples: Elavil, imipramine, Norpramin)
- antihistamines (example: Benadryl)
- atypical antidepressants (examples: Serzone, Trazadone)
- beta-blockers (example: Propanolol)
- miscellaneous (examples: Buspar, Neurontin)

New antidepressants (those introduced in North America since the 1980s) such as Effexor have for the most part replaced tricyclics and MAOIs as treatment for both depression and most anxiety disorders. These new antidepressants are actually safer, though the main reason the tricyclics are still in use is their lower cost.

How Each Class of Medicines Works Inside the Brain

Benzodiazepines

Benzodiazepines work by acting on a neurotransmitter GABA. GABA's function is to quiet down the postsynaptic neuron, and in so doing, it inhibits that neuron's ability to conduct a neural impulse or send the message on to the next neuron. Benzodiazepines strengthen GABA's ability to quiet down the neurons, leaving them

insomniacs: People who have an inability to sleep.

residual effect: An effect that remains after the purpose for which the drug has been prescribed has been completed.

relaxed. In this way, benzodiazepines help anxious people calm down. Because the benzodiazepine drugs act very quickly (as quickly as one hour, unlike some other categories of drugs used to treat anxiety disorders, which can take several weeks to work) these drugs can also be used to treat insomniacs, allowing people to take one an hour before bedtime, sleep a full night, and wake up with little or no residual effect.

Antidepressants

Antidepressants work in a different way. As stated earlier, neurotransmitters such as noradrenaline and serotonin can be reabsorbed into the presynaptic neuron after binding to their receptors on the postsynaptic neuron. If that reabsorption (also called reuptake) can be stopped, then the life of the neurotransmitter can be

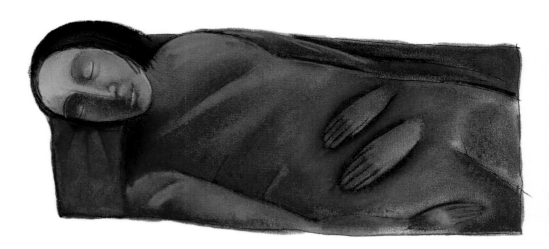

Benzodiazepines act on a person's neurotransmitters, causing her to relax and become sleepy.

When a person is experiencing extreme psychiatric symptoms, benzodiazepines offer a fast-acting treatment.

Psychiatric drugs are powerful chemicals and should always be used with caution.

prolonged. The neurotransmitter can reattach to the receptor in the post-synaptic neuron, making the transmission of the message even stronger. Antidepressants such as Prozac, Paxil, and Zoloft (SSRIs) specifically block the reuptake of the neurotransmitter serotonin.

Some antidepressants also block the receptors for acetylcholine, another neurotransmitter, but these anticholinergic drugs can cause side effects such as dry mouth, constipation, blurry vision, and difficulty in urination. Other antidepressant drugs block the alpha receptor, a receptor found on blood vessels, with the result that a person may become dizzy and light-headed when standing up quickly due to lowered blood pressure.

Once a neurotransmitter falls back into the synapse, it can be broken down by enzymes and made into waste material. MAOIs (such as Nardil and Eldepryl) act by reducing one of these enzymes, thus allowing the neurotransmitter to last longer in the synapse.

Antipsychotics

These drugs (such as Thorazine, Haldol, and Prolixin) are used to treat the psychotic symptoms, such as delusions and hallucinations, that occur primarily in people with schizophrenia. They block the neurotransmitter dopamine's ability to bind to the dopamine receptor. This means that when the presynaptic neuron tries to send a nerve signal that depends on the neurotransmitter dopamine, the receptor on the post-synaptic neuron is blocked by the antipsychotic drug. The dopamine, left in the synapse and unable to carry on the signal, is partly taken back up into the presynaptic neuron and partly degraded by enzymes. The message, or nerve signal, is unable to get through.

Twenty-first–century medical practitioners often use medication to help them "unravel" complicated mental conditions.

Clearly, neurons are vital to our functioning. What's more, neurons are irreplaceable. While other areas of the body, such as skin or hair, replace dead cells with new cells of the same type, the brain is different. It has always been thought that, once the brain or the spinal cord is injured, those injuries are permanent, because once neurons die, the body does not make new neurons, but some scientists are now calling into question that information.

Monoamine Oxidase Inhibitors (MAOIs)

MAOIs, such as Nardil and Eldepryl, operate by inhibiting the breakdown of some neurotransmitters inside the presynaptic neuron.

Scientists who research the drugs and disorders discussed in this book emphasize that anxiety disorders are far more complex than we can understand right now. Although it appears logical to say that if increasing the amount of serotonin and noradrenaline in the synapse relieves the symptoms of depression, then depression must be caused by a lack of these neurotransmitters, the truth appears to be far more involved and complex than that.

How complex is it? Gorman explains that researchers have now learned that the sensitivity of the postsynaptic neuron's receptors is affected by many different factors. For instance, if these receptors are "starved" of the neurotransmitter for a time, they develop a **supersensitivity** to that neurotransmitter the next time they receive it. The post-synaptic neuron may also produce new receptors. Transmitting neural messages involves a complicated chain of chemical reactions, involving chemicals known as "second messengers" working within the postsynaptic cell.

supersensitivity: An exaggerated response to medication.

"Scientists now believe that we may understand only the tip of the iceberg about how neurotransmitters work," Gorman writes; he goes on to say that as the details are worked out, more psychiatric drugs with very specific actions and very few side effects will be developed.

Experts admit that we don't have a complete concept of how the brain operates at a cellular level, and as yet, we have an almost total lack of understanding of how the brain as a whole is organized. Even though we do not yet completely comprehend how the brain operates, doctors can still observe and treat on the basis of what they know now. We may not have full understanding, but clearly, many of the drugs described here have a beneficial effect on patients suffering from anxiety disorders. These drugs make it possible for these people to lead a relatively normal, productive life.

A traumatic event like a car accident can lead to posttraumatic stress disorder.

Chapter Six

Risks and Side Effects

The day Gerald left his family's small dairy farm in northern Michigan to attend the University of Michigan in Ann Arbor on an academic scholarship, he felt his life was really beginning. The town of Ann Arbor itself seemed a whirl of activity to him and that didn't even include the excitement of life at a major university. He went from a high school graduating class of forty-three to a freshman university class of thousands.

One of the activities he was introduced to at the university, however, was drinking. Back home, in a small community where everyone knew him, Gerald could never have gotten away with underage drinking. Here in the city, though, many of his new friends drank routinely.

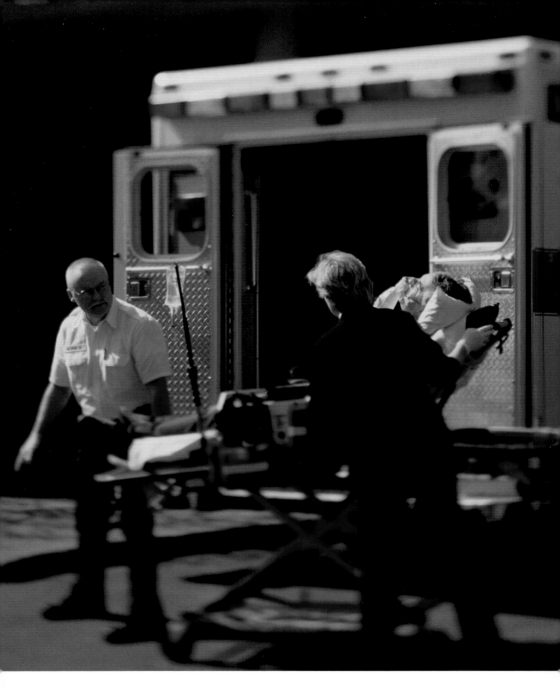

Emergency workers will attend to an accident victim's immediate physical needs, but the psychiatric damage may be far more long lasting.

One Friday night just three weeks into the semester, Gerald found himself headed to a party with his roommate Rob and a new friend named Lisa. Rob swore he hadn't been drinking before he got behind the wheel of the car, but Gerald felt sure he could smell alcohol on Rob's breath. After Rob drove for just a few minutes, his judgment was obviously not what it should have been. Gerald was still working up the courage to tell Rob to pull over and let him drive—after all, he didn't want to make a fool of himself in front of Lisa—when Rob decided he could beat an oncoming train.

By the time Gerald and Lisa realized what Rob was going to do, it was too late to stop him. Gerald heard Lisa's screams of terror for only a few agonizing seconds before he was thrown clear of the car on impact; then everything went black.

Gerald had a broken collarbone, but he lived. Everyone said his survival was miraculous. He felt the situation was far from a miracle, however. From the minute he heard that both Rob and Lisa had been killed, he felt as though he'd been plunged into the worst nightmare he'd ever known—a nightmare from which he couldn't wake up.

For the first twenty-four hours after he regained consciousness in the hospital, his mind seemed to settle on one thought and stay there—"I should have done something sooner. I should've made Rob stop." That was bad enough, but what happened next was even worse. When coverage of Lisa's funeral came on the local TV news, he lay watching from his hospital bed. Suddenly, he was there again in the car, terrified of the oncoming train, frozen by Lisa's high-pitched screams.

When Gerald came out of his flash-back, nurses were hovering over him, adjusting his **intravenous** medications and trying to keep him still in the bed. He had no idea where he was.

After that, Gerald began experiencing one flashback after another. Long after his collarbone had healed, the flashbacks were ruining his college

> **intravenous:** Something, often medication, given through the vein.

career. He'd gone home for a few weeks to the dairy farm to finish healing, but once he was back on campus, he found he could no longer concentrate on his studies. He couldn't pass any of the tests and couldn't seem to complete even the shortest homework assignment. He had to do better than this—much better—or he would lose his scholarship. And if that happened, there was no way his family could afford to pay his tuition at the university.

Above and beyond the guilt that always weighed on his mind, he had to contend with the flashbacks . . . those menacing, terrorizing

Noises often trigger PTSD flashbacks.

A person with PTSD may not be able to concentrate. The demands of normal life may seem to be overwhelming.

moments when he didn't just remember the deadly crash, he felt he was actually there. Gerald's dormitory room faced a busy intersection, and several times the screech of brakes outside woke him from a sound sleep directly into a flashback. He began to be afraid to even fall asleep.

By the time finals drew near in December, Gerald could no longer remember how he felt back in the days when he was not tired all the time. He was always exhausted, but he couldn't seem to sit still long enough to rest. Concentrating on anything—let alone an hour-long lecture by a slow-talking professor—became a bigger chore than he could handle. Feeling that he could no longer cope with all the demands of university life, Gerald began to consider dropping out of school. Only the thought of how disappointed his parents would be kept him from doing so before the end of the semester.

His one hope was that Christmas break would be a time to relax and get back to what he vaguely remembered as "normal." Most of all, he hoped he could sleep. He felt sure that if he could just get a few nights of sound sleep he would be able to cope. However, Christmas break turned out to be a disaster. Unable to relax, worrying about the upcoming second semester, Gerald found himself unable to sleep any more than he had on campus. Instead, he lay awake for hours, struggling with the fear of falling asleep, only to drift into sleep and be wakened into yet another flashback. The milking, the animals, the equipment—everything on the farm now seemed to irritate him, and he was ashamed of how often he snapped at his brothers.

Gerald did return to the university for the second semester, but only because he didn't know what else to do. How could he disappoint his parents by dropping out? Yet how could he continue to function under this kind of stress? One of his main concerns was that if he told anyone what was happening, they might think he was crazy.

Finally, at the end of his first week back in Ann Arbor, Gerald stumbled into the campus clinic and asked to see a doctor. Gerald described what was going on and all but begged for help.

"You should have come sooner," Dr. Barnes told him. "We have medicines now that can help with post-traumatic stress disorder."

Gerald looked at him, puzzled. "Isn't that what the soldiers got? After the Vietnam War?"

Dr. Barnes nodded. "Yes, but they aren't the only ones." He explained briefly about PTSD, prescribed some medication called Xanax (alprazolam) and warned Gerald not to use alcohol at all while taking it, because the combination could be deadly. He then recommended that Gerald see a therapist in town.

Very quickly, Gerald began to notice a lessening of his anxiety and then of his flashbacks. By the time he'd been on the Xanax for three weeks, he was also seeing a psychotherapist on campus twice a week, a man with whom he felt free to talk about his symptoms and anxiety. With the help of his medication and therapy, Gerald began to feel more relaxed, more confident that he could get through the day without another flashback.

Then, after Gerald had been on Xanax a few months, the psychotherapist informed Gerald that it was time to go off his medication. Gerald was startled, and a little frightened, imagining life without it. The therapist assured him that they would take it slowly, tapering the medicine gradually.

"But it has to be done, Gerald. Xanax, like all the medicines in this class of drugs, is habit forming."

Drugs offer effective treatment options to people with anxiety disorders—but they should always be used with caution.

What is a side effect?

Dr. Jack Gorman gives a simple summary of what a drug side effect is: "A side effect is anything a drug does that we don't want it to do," and explains that any chemical substance we put into our bodies will affect more than just the one part of our body we want it to affect. He likens this to the food we eat, using a steak as an example of good taste and a good source of needed protein for our bodies. He then points out that steak can do other things to our bodies, however, including increasing our cholesterol level and adding unwanted weight. Some people will consider both these positive and negative effects of eating steak and decide to go ahead and eat the steak because the benefits outweigh the risks. In much the same way, drugs can provide needed benefits but also produce unwanted side effects, though some may be much more serious than the "side effects" of eating steak. And in some cases, the benefits will outweigh the side effects to the degree that many people suffering from anxiety disorders will decide they will take the drugs and find ways to deal with the side effects.

Gerald's symptoms, including his anxiety, insomnia, irritability, and flashbacks, began to return quickly after he began to cut back on the Xanax. Added to those symptoms were new ones from going off the medicine: diarrhea and confusion. The situation became more than he could handle, and Gerald finally had to return to his hometown where he went to a doctor who switched him to a non-habit-forming SSRI. Because of the side effects of the drug he'd been prescribed, more than a year went by before Gerald was able to return to his studies, which he pursued at a local community college.

Many psychiatric drugs may cause unwanted weight gain.

What Causes Side Effects?

Side effects are caused for the most part when drugs affect neurotransmitters and receptors that are not involved in any way with the illness at question. When Carmella first began taking Elavil (amitriptyline) for her anxiety disorder, she noticed within just a few days that her heart was beating much faster than it had been before, but she did not relate this to her medication. One day, when Carmella was in a meeting with her boss, her heart was racing. It then began beating erratically, and Carmella grew dizzy. She excused herself

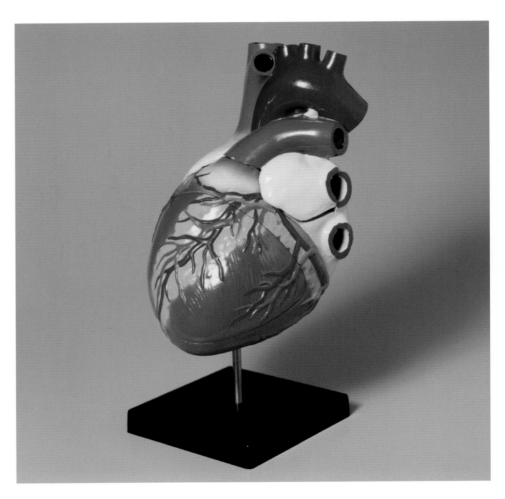

Psychiatric drugs can affect heart function.

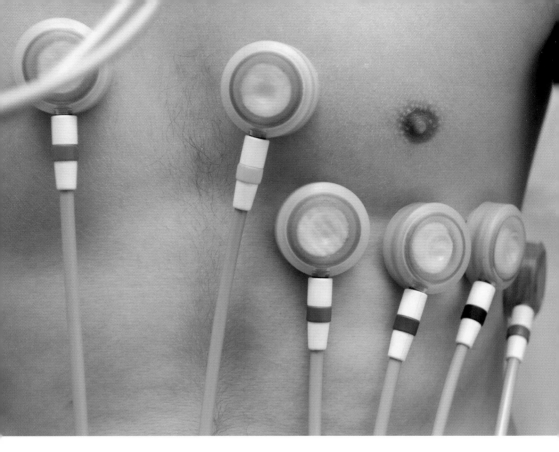

EKGs are used to detect and monitor heart disease.

from the meeting as soon as possible; since the erratic beating and dizziness were growing worse, she went directly to the emergency room.

There, as is common with heart-related complaints, Carmella was rushed immediately into a treatment room, given an EKG, and hooked up to a heart monitor. A nurse asked many questions, recording Carmella's answers on a chart, then asked her to list all medications she was taking. When the doctor entered the treatment room a few minutes later, he immediately began questioning Carmella further about the amitriptyline.

EKG: Electrocardiogram; a test used to diagnose heart disease.

After she finished answering, the doctor asked, "Did anyone tell you, when you started on this medicine, that it could cause heart arrhythmias?"

Carmella shook her head.

"You didn't happen to read the package insert that came with your prescription, did you?" he asked.

Again she shook her head. "I just figured that if a doctor prescribed something for me it'd be safe."

The doctor shook his head. "It will be as safe as possible, but that doesn't mean you'll never experience side effects—some minor, some possibly serious. It's important that you read all

arrhythmias:
Alterations in the heart's rhythm, sometimes caused by medications. In some cases the arrhythmias are not serious, but some arrhythmias, especially sudden-onset ones, can cause death.

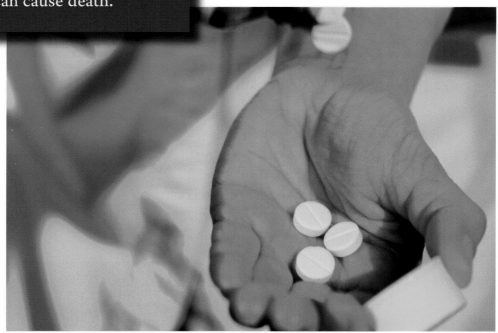

If you are taking a psychiatric medication, you need to understand any and all possible side effects.

the information, ask questions, and educate yourself as much as possible about anything you put into your body. That gives you a much better chance of staying safe and healthy."

Carmella was taken off amitriptyline immediately, and after her heart returned to its normal rate and rhythm, she returned to her doctor to discuss another medication for her anxiety disorder.

Possible Side Effects of Drugs Used to Treat Anxiety Disorders

Medications for anxiety disorders fall into the following groups, with possible side effects noted for each group:

Benzodiazepines

- sedation
- poor physical coordination
- memory impairment

When used daily for months:

- dulled emotions
- impairment of cognitive skills
- contribute to depression
- habit forming

Selective Serotonin Reuptake Inhibitors (SSRIs)

- fatigue
- occasionally cause agitation
- decreased sexual drive/impaired sexual response

Tricyclic Antidepressants [TCAs]

- weight gain
- dry mouth
- constipation
- sweating
- light-headedness due to low blood pressure
- fast heart rate
- visual disturbances
- confusion
- urinary retention

Monoamine Oxidase Inhibitors [MAOIs]

- weight gain
- dry mouth
- insomnia
- impaired sexual response
- light-headedness due to low blood pressure
- potential to cause a stroke if taken with adrenaline or adrenaline-like substances (found in cough/cold medicines, food products such as aged cheese and processed meats)

Buspirone

- nausea
- dizziness
- drowsiness
- headache
- nervousness
- insomnia
- dry mouth

Trazodone

- sedation
- weight gain
- dry mouth
- gastrointestinal disturbance
- blurred vision
- tremor
- low blood pressure

Gabapentin

- sedation
- dizziness
- tremor
- hostility
- visual disturbances

All prescription drug use must be combined with educated aware-ness on the part of the consumer since every drug carries both the potential for benefit and for harm. Patients protect themselves by reading and understanding the informational inserts that come with their prescriptions and by reporting to their physician all medica-tions they are using, including herbs and "natural" compounds.

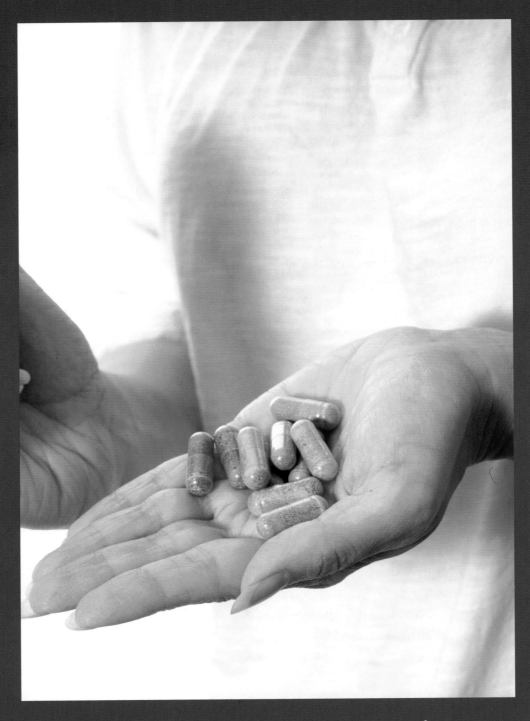

Diet and vitamins can play a role in treatment for anxiety disorders.

Chapter Seven

Alternative and Supplementary Treatments

Lifestyle changes can do a great deal of good in the management of anxiety disorders, but these changes must be adhered to diligently in order to make a lasting difference. Following is an overview of some of the changes recommended by Edward Drummond, M.D., in his book *The Complete Guide to Psychiatric Drugs*, in dealing with anxiety disorders.

Diet

Drummond stresses the importance of eating balanced meals three to four times per day and emphasizes the need to avoid eating products that are high in sugar. Since the body's energy is provided by converting food to glucose, or blood sugar, when that blood sugar level is allowed to fall, the adrenal gland releases the hormone adrenaline. Adrenaline not only increases blood sugar but also causes the increased heart rate, palpitations, sweating, and the inner feeling of restlessness common to anxiety.

Because the diet affects the blood glucose level, it also indirectly affects the amount of adrenaline the body produces. If a person goes without eating for more than four hours, the glucose

Relaxation techniques can help reduce and control anxious feelings.

Relaxation Training

Relaxation training is a technique that helps people who suffer from anxiety. When we feel anxious, our bodies automatically respond by tensing muscles. This is the explanation for many of the headaches people suffer. When the temporalis muscle that surrounds the skull tightens, it can cause both stabbing and dull pain.

Patients learning this technique sit in a comfortable chair in a quiet room. There they learn to tense each muscle group in sequence, as tightly as possible, and then relax them, from the feet and lower legs, to the upper leg, the abdomen, the chest, then hands, arms, shoulders, neck, and head and facial muscles. Patients perform this once or twice a day for several weeks, by which time they are able to recognize readily when their muscles are tense. People who suffer from anxiety often suffer also from chronic muscle tension, and this exercise not only helps them recognize the tension, but also to relax, which often reduces the headaches and backaches common to some anxiety disorders.

Adapted from *The New Psychiatry*, by Jack M. Gorman, M.D.

level falls, causing the adrenaline to increase, and along with it, the symptoms we associate with anxiety. Food high in sugar causes an initial elevation in blood sugar, but the levels fall rapidly, which also increases adrenaline and anxiety symptoms.

Balanced meals, including whole grains, vegetables, and some protein, allow the body to maintain more even glucose levels, leading to less adrenaline production, and thus, less anxiety symptoms.

Drugs

Consider cutting out caffeine, alcohol, and tobacco use completely. Anxiety sufferers can notice an immediate decrease in the intensity of anxiety when caffeine is stopped. Cutting out alcohol is also important, as its continued use can increase anxiety symptoms. Some people notice an increase in anxiety when they stop tobacco, though the change will ultimately have good results.

Exercise

Exercise causes the release of adrenaline, which actually helps enable the body to do the exercise. After the exercise is finished, adrenaline production is reduced. Drummond also points out that people who exercise get used to the feelings of a higher heart rate, palpitations, and perspiration, which may help them put up with the physical symptoms of anxiety.

Relaxation Techniques

Exercises that make you feel calmer are often used as relaxation techniques. Such exercises include deep-breathing exercises, yoga, meditation, muscle relaxation exercises (see sidebar, page 113) and tapes, and biofeedback. Practiced throughout the day on a regular basis, such exercises and techniques can help people maintain a calm feeling when they face situations that formerly produced anxiety.

Psychotherapy

Before psychiatric drugs became popular to combat anxiety disorders, psychotherapy was the most often used treatment. Many people envision only the old scenario of a psychiatrist in a chair, taking notes, while a patient lying on a couch talks on and on. However, psychotherapy now takes many different forms.

Yoga is an effective relaxation technique.

classical conditioning: Establishing new behavior as a result of psychological modifications of stumuli responses.

operant conditioning: The process by which the results of a person's behavior determine if it is likely to recur.

Group and individual therapy are available in the following categories: behavioral (based on principles of **classical** and **operant conditioning**), cognitive (designed to change faulty beliefs and assumptions, and restructure distorted thinking), interpersonal (designed to correct faulty relationship patterns), and psychodynamic (therapy with a more actively involved therapist).

Many people have overcome anxiety disorders with the help of alternative therapies. When Roberto started high school, he

Alternative medicine—like acupuncture and natural remedies—offers other options to people with psychiatric and physical disorders.

If she suspects you have a psychiatric disorder, your medical practitioner can refer you to a psychologist or psychiatrist.

suddenly found himself struggling to a much greater degree with a problem that had always bothered him throughout his earlier years of school. In middle school, he had noticed that whenever he faced a quiz or an exam, he tensed up and struggled to remember the information he had studied so diligently the night before. Now, though, he felt as though his brain simply froze at the prospect of a test. Even the anticipation of a quiz the next day was enough to completely overwhelm him with anxiety, to the point of making him feel dizzy and break into a cold sweat.

"What's happening with you?" the school counselor asked. "Your grade point average has dropped to a 'D'—not exactly the kind of work you were doing in middle school."

Roberto shrugged and hung his head. "I don't know what's wrong. I just can't do the tests. I study and study, and I know all the answers at home. Then I get here and—." He spread his hands to either side, palms up in a gesture of hopelessness. "It's like brain freeze. My mind goes blank, I start sweating all over and the room starts spinning . . ."

The counselor leaned forward, elbows on her desk. "I think I may know what's going on here, Roberto. Would you be willing to see the school psychologist?"

"Yeah, I guess so," Roberto answered. "I have to do something, or I'm gonna fail this year."

When Roberto started meeting with the psychologist, it gradually became evident that he was struggling with negative feelings about his father, a brilliant university physics professor who routinely belittled Roberto's performance at school. Once Roberto recognized that his strong negative feelings toward his father were the basis for his problems with testing, the way was cleared for him to begin working on practical ways of coping with his problem.

His psychologist might then have Roberto undergo a form of exposure therapy, which would involved having Roberto face, or imagine facing, an exam. Systematic desensitization (see chapter four), developed by psychiatrist Joseph Wolpe in 1958, showed that "learned fear responses could be unlearned if the person confronted the feared stimulus or situation while relaxed," according to Richard S. Perrotto and Joseph Culkin, in *Exploring Abnormal Psychology*.

The school psychologist, Roberto's father, and teachers together came up with a plan that would allow Roberto to be assessed in other ways than through tests, while at the same time he continued to work steadily with the psychologist to overcome his fear of testing. Eventually, Roberto was able to resolve his anxiety and begin taking tests again without experiencing intense symptoms of panic. Through this experience, Roberto's father began to understand just how much negative pressure he had been putting on his son, and the two were able to talk more freely and develop a closer father–son relationship.

In the event of an anxiety disorder such as Cassie McCauley's panic disorder, the attacks were frightening and needed to be controlled quickly. To this end, medication can be used as described in

Tension between family members can contribute to increased feelings of anxiety.

Extracts of the plant Rhodiola rosea have only recently appeared in the North American herbal market. However, people as far back as the Vikings have been taking the herb (usually in the form of tea) for its perceived physical and mental benefits. In Russia, soldiers attempting to reduce stress and boost their energy drank tea made from the root of Rhodiola rosea. Today, numerous studies are being conducted on this herb, its possible benefits, and its possible side effects. Researchers now believe that its benefits may be the result of a number of chemical reactions including reduction of the stress hormone cortisol, an increase in hormones that positively affect mood, and a surge in the molecule adenosine triphosphate, which cells use for energy.

the earlier chapters of this book to bring the attacks under control. Some doctors then recommend combining the medication with cognitive/behavioral therapy. For other anxiety disorders, such as specific phobia, cognitive/behavioral therapy is usually the first recommendation. As with Trevor Anhalt, the trigger for his fear (flying in airplanes) was simply not present in his life on a regular enough basis to require his being on medication day in and day out. In this situation, doctors will often do exactly what Trevor's doctor did: prescribe a short-term and fast-acting medication to help the patient face a specific difficult situation, but also recommend cognitive/behavioral therapy to aid the patient in overcoming the phobia permanently.

This type of cognitive/behavioral therapy typically involves exposure and desensitization. An understanding therapist would gradually expose Trevor to the very situation that terrified him, perhaps through pictures at first then through exposure to a model of the inside of a plane. Next, Trevor might be required to enter a plane that was simply sitting at the airport. In this way, he would be gradually exposed to more and more of the actual experience of flying in a

"Natural" substances offer alternatives to medication. However, natural remedies also contain chemicals and should be used with care.

plane, and he would gradually become less and less sensitive to this particular phobic object.

Alternative remedies for anxiety disorders also include herbs, vitamins, and dietary supplements, some of which have been used for centuries by people around the world. The Food and Drug Administration in the United States regulates the prescription drugs used by psychiatrists and other doctors for the treatment of anxiety disorders, which means that these drugs must pass a rigorous series of trials before they can be advertised and claims can be made for their effectiveness. This is not the case with alternative remedies, and Edward Drummond, M.D., and other medical doctors caution consumers to remember that any chemical compound taken to alter the physical

Homeopathic Treatment
for Anxiety Disorders

Homeopathy is a form of alternative medicine that looks at disease and disorders from a very different perspective from conventional medicine. It looks at a person's entire physical and mental being, rather than dividing a patient into various symptoms and disorders. Homeopathic medicine uses tiny doses to stimulate the body's ability to heal itself. In some cases, these doses may be administered only once every few months or years.

According to Judyth Reichenberg-Ullman and Robert Ullman, authors of several books on homeopathic medicine, homeopathy offers safe, natural alternatives that can supplement or replace conventional pharmaceutical treatment. Homeopathic treatments should be used only after consulting with a licensed practitioner.

or mental state is a drug. This includes caffeine, alcohol, and nicotine; it also includes vitamin C, multivitamins, and herbs. With all of these substances, there is the possibility of drug interaction and the potential for negative side effects. "Any substance that can cause an alteration in one body system can cause alterations in others. There is no drug that has only beneficial effects," says Drummond.

With those cautions in mind, the following remedies are sometimes used for mild symptoms of anxiety, as their effects are subtle.

Chamomile, derived from the flower of the herb, is thought to interact with the same receptors used by benzodiazepine drugs. It may also affect the histamine system, but could cause allergic reactions.

Hops, a vine that grows both in Europe and the Americas, is used for both anxiety and insomnia and seems to have a mild sedative

Homeopathic practitioners prescribe natural substances to treat physical and mental conditions.

action. It must be used cautiously when combined with other sedatives, including alcohol.

Kava was first used by South Pacific Islanders. The plant is a member of the pepper family and is used for treatment of anxiety, although how it works is unknown. Kava has actually been proven more effective than a placebo in treating anxiety. It should not be used by people who are depressed, and it can make symptoms of Parkinson's disease worse. Great caution should be exercised when kava is used with alcohol or other sedating drugs since the combination may have too strong a sedating effect. Kava should not be used for more than three months, except under a doctor's guidance. According to Drummond, side effects of extended use include yellow skin, muscle spasms, biochemical abnormalities, vision disturbances, and shortness of breath.

Lemon balm, a member of the mint family, is thought to possibly be helpful for anxiety though there are no studies proving this. No side effects are reported, but caution should be exercised when lemon balm is used with other sedatives, such as alcohol.

Passionflower, a vine, grows in both North and South America. It is used for anxiety and insomnia and should be used with special caution with other sedatives such as alcohol. Side effects include allergic reactions.

Saint-John's-wort, also known as Hypericum, grows both in Europe and the United States. Its active ingredient appears to be hypericin, which acts on the neurotransmitters serotonin, norepinephrine, dopamine, and GABA. It also lowers levels of cortisol (a hormone). Many studies in Europe have proven that Saint-John's-wort helps relieve mild to moderate depression, and some reports show it can help with anxiety. It must not be used with other antidepressants and can cause a person to sunburn more easily than they normally would. Side effects of Saint-John's-wort include the excessive sensitivity to sunlight mentioned above, constipation, restlessness, sedation, dry mouth, dizziness, and indigestion.

Valerian grows both in Europe and the United States and binds with GABA, which is the same receptor affected by the benzodiazepines. Numerous studies show valerian to be affective for insomnia, and it is also used for anxiety. Although valerian is very similar to the benzodiazepines, there is no evidence to date that it is habit forming; it does not have the side effects common to those drugs, namely daytime sedation, depression, and memory impairment. There have been, however, some reports of people having headaches and unexpected stimulant effects.

Anxiety disorders can cause serious dysfunction in everyday life, as Cassie, Trevor, Charlene, and Tara all discovered. As these disorders become more widely recognized and new treatments are developed, more and more people are learning that anxiety disorders do not have to stand in the way of a full and productive life.

Further Reading

Bourne, Edmund J. *The Anxiety and Phobia Workbook*. Oakland, Calif.: New Harbinger Publications, 2010.

Clark, David A. and Christine Purdon. *Overcoming Obsessive Thoughts*. Oakland, Calif.: New Harbinger Publications, 2005.

Daitch, Carolyn. *Anxiety Disorders: The Go-to Guide for Clients and Therapists*. New York: W.W. Norton & Company, 2011.

Drummond, Edward. *The Complete Guide to Psychiatric Drugs*. New York: John Wiley & Sons, 2006.

Gorman, Jack M. *The Essential Guide to Psychiatric Drugs*. New York: St. Martin's Press, 2007.

Gorman, Jack M. *The New Psychiatry*. New York: St. Martin's Press, 1996.

For More Information

National Mental Health Association
www.nmha.org

American Psychological Association
www.apa.org

American Psychiatric Association
www.psych.org

Anxiety Disorders Association of America
www.adaa.org

National Anxiety Foundation
www.lexington-on-line.com/naf.html

Publisher's Note:
The websites listed on this page were active at the time of publication. The publisher is not responsible for websites that have changed their address or discontinued operation since the date of publication. The publisher will review and update the websites upon each reprint.

Index

About the Author & Consultants

Shirley Brinkerhoff was a writer, editor, speaker, and musician. She published six young adult novels, six informational books for young people, scores of short stories and articles, and taught at writers' conferences throughout the United States.

Mary Ann McDonnell, Ph.D., R.N., is the owner of South Shore Psychiatric Services, where she provides psychiatric services to children and adolescents. She has worked as a psychiatric nurse at Franciscan Hospital for Children and has been a clinical instructor for Northeastern University and Boston College advanced-practice nursing students. She was also the director of clinical trials in the pediatric psychopharmacology research unit at Massachusetts General Hospital. Her areas of expertise are bipolar disorder in children and adolescents, ADHD, and depression.

Donald Esherick has worked in regulatory affairs at Rhone-Poulenc Rorer, Wyeth Pharmaceuticals, Pfizer, and Pharmalink Consulting. He specializes in the chemistry section (manufacture and testing) of investigational and marketed drugs.